Speak, Lord

Lynn Steward

All rights reserved. No part of this publication may be reproduced, stored in a retrieval system or transmitted, in any form or by any means without the prior permission in writing of the author or as expressly permitted by law, or under terms agreed with the appropriate reprographics rights organisation.

Enquiries concerning reproduction outside the scope of the above should be sent to the author. You must not circulate this book in any other binding or cover, and you must impose this same condition on any acquirer.

Copyright © 2024 Lynn Steward
All Rights Reserved
ISBN 9798343865875

Acknowledgements:

My thanks go to my patient husband, Mike, for deciphering my pencil scribbles and putting them into printed text.

To Susan Harryman, who prepared everything for publishing.

To my son, Andy, for once again providing a lovely cover photograph.

And finally, to everyone who bought my first book, *A Still Small Voice*, and encouraged me so much.

Introduction

I wrote my first book, *A Still Small Voice,* in lockdown during the COVID pandemic. At that time, I spent longer with God than was my usual habit and felt that each day He gave me words from Himself to write down. This I did, day by day, and eventually had 366 (one for the leap year). At the end of this time, I imagined that I would return to my previous way of sitting with the Lord. However, the next day I was surprised to receive more thoughts and words to write. This continued day by day and it seemed to me that this could be a second book.

However, I realized that these words were longer and could not be in the same format as the previous book. Thus, it occurred to me to make it different.

Furthermore, after 130 days, I ceased to get "words" from the Lord each day! Therefore, I quote two scriptures, highlight a prayer, and propose three questions for the reader. The point of the questions is really to challenge us, not to be just hearers of the word, but doers also (James 1:22) - challenging us as to what it is that God is saying and what we should do as a result of these words. I have left space after each question should you wish to clarify your thinking. I always find it helps to write things down!

As disciples of Jesus, it behooves us to be active and ready to follow his guidance. Most importantly, to reach others by whatever means with the gospel-the good news that Jesus loves us died for our sins and rose again defeating death (1 Peter 2:24; 2 Timothy 1:10).

I hope and pray that this book will be an encouragement to you and that it will spur you on to love and good works (Hebrews 10: 24).

As a footnote, I have been greatly encouraged by many cards comments and texts saying how helpful my book has been. Here are a few examples -

" Each morning I am so eager to hear what God has to say." Sophie C

"It' s amazing how often it just hits the right note." Brenda S

"This book has opened my eyes to understand that I am truly loved by God, despite my failings , and the importance of reading the Bible". S.C.

"I shall treasure your book and read it from cover to cover" Gina.
And many more….

1: God's Great Love

I first loved you. I chose you to become part of My family. I adopted you and made you my own. I redeemed you from the enemy who had taken you for himself. I paid for you with My own blood, shed on the cross. I was wounded and bloodied for your sins to be forgiven and taken away; dying in your place that you may have life - abundant and eternal.

Now, I ask you to live for Me. Live a life of love, firstly for Me and then for others. Love as I love, not just those who are good and kind to you, but love those who are opposed to you. True love conquers all things, and a soft answer turns away anger.

Be an overcomer. Overcome lies with the truth, fear with faith and unbelief with trust in Me alone. Take up your sword and shield and fight for what is good and right and truthful. Do not seek to flee from the enemy but stand your ground and resist him and he will flee from you. Overcome him with the word of your testimony and by proclaiming the power that comes from the shed blood of the Lamb.

You will eat from the Tree of Life and will dwell with Me forever.

Scripture:

We love Him because He first loved us. 1 John 4:19.

They overcame him (Satan) by the blood of the Lamb and by the word of their testimony. Revelation 12:11.

Prayer

Lord, I can never thank You enough for Your great love towards me. Love that took You to the cross to die in my place. Today I ask for strength from You to overcome the lies of the enemy and to live a life of love. Amen.

Questions:

1. What does it mean to you that you are a Child of God?

2. Who can you show love to today?

3. What do you need to overcome?

2: The Word of God

My word is living and Powerful. It is sharper than any double-edged sword. It is able to convict of sin and righteousness and the judgement to come. The strength of My word uncovers the state of your soul and spirit. Firstly, it shows the great need of a Saviour from your sinful life. Secondly, it demonstrates the right way to live a new life, and one that is consecrated for My purposes.

As you declare My word, it reaches into the heavenly realms where the battle against evil is being fought by My holy angels. Declarations from My word of worship and praise of Me are powerful for bringing down strongholds. Never underestimate what can be achieved by the power of the word.

When I was tempted by Satan in the wilderness, My response to each one was, "it is written". Satan had no power, no answer and was forced to flee. Learn from this account and keep your own sword at the ready, keenly sharpened for attack against the enemy. Do not just hold your ground but advance and take enemy ground.

How do you keep your sword fit for purpose? By dwelling in My word, meditating upon it and making it part of your life. Be armed and ready and you will not fall into temptation. Instead, you will be able to fight the good fight of faith and great will be your reward.

Scripture:

"For the word of God is living and active and sharper than any double-edged sword." Hebrews 4:12.

Jesus answered, "it is written, man shall not live by bread alone". Matthew 4:4.

Prayer

Thank You Lord, for Your word, the Bible. Give me a hunger for it that I may know You more and understand Your ways. May it be a sword in my hand to defeat the schemes of the enemy. Amen.

Questions:

1. What scripture can you put in your armoury today?

2. How valuable do you find the word of God?

3. How often do you read it?

3: The Guilt of Sin

Don't walk about carrying a load that is guilt. If you say you have not sinned, you are a liar, all have sinned and fallen short of My glory. Accept the fact of your sin, confess it to Me and receive the forgiveness that I long to give.

It was for this very reason that I came to the Earth, to deal with sin and death. If you confess your sin, I am faithful and just and will forgive you and cleanse you from all unrighteousness.

I bore the sin of the world in My own body on the cross. The shedding of blood, My blood, was necessary to be the living perfect sacrifice. It was the final and unblemished offering for sin, once and forever.
If you continue to carry your guilt it negates that work that I did on the cross. I died to bring you freedom from guilt and shame. Therefore, appropriate this freedom and pass all that guilt and shame over to Me. Walk in freedom, I have set you free. I have opened the prison door which held you captive to sin so that you can live for Me. Cherish your newness of life and live a life worthy of your calling, a child of God. Bear the fruit from My Holy Spirit and may My Kingdom come, and My will be done on earth as in heaven.

Scripture:

"who Himself bore our sins in His own body on the tree, that we, having died to sins, might live for righteousness". 1 Peter 2:24.

*"If we confess our sins, He is faithful and just to forgive us our sins and to cleanse us from all unrighteousness".
1 John 1:9.*

Prayer

Lord, please forgive me for the times that I carry my guilt instead of coming to You to confess and find forgiveness.
Thank You that You came to open the prison door of guilt and shame and allow me to walk in freedom. Amen.

Questions:

1. Are you holding onto any guilt?

2. Do you think that you alone are unworthy of God's forgiveness?

3. Can you accept this forgiveness and truly forgive yourself today?

4: The Power of the Holy Spirit

At times you walk in a dry and thirsty land. When you walk according to your fleshly desires, your soul and spirit within cry out for the refreshing of My Holy Spirit. You were made for fellowship with Me and not the world. Works done in the flesh will not endure for eternity or receive my reward. Therefore, take heed to your life and not pander to the desires of the flesh. Rather look to Me. Ask to be filled daily with My Holy Spirit that you may know the rivers of living water that I can provide to renew and refresh you.

Living in this world is not your true home. You are really on a pilgrimage to Heaven. Thus, you need My strength to endure the battles, the tribulation and trials that will inevitably come upon you. Remember that I am with you always. I will never leave you. My Holy Spirit within can comfort, strengthen and uphold you so that you do not become dry and thirsty. My rivers of living water are not only for your well-being but that through you, My Kingdom may be extended and My will be done on earth as in heaven. Ask and it shall be given you, seek and you will find Me, knock and the door will be open to you. Drink deeply of the water of life.

Scripture:

"Ask and it will be given you, seek and you will find, knock and it will be open to you." Matthew 7:7.

"If you then, being evil, know how to give good gifts to your children how much more will your heavenly Father give the Holy Spirit to those who ask Him." Luke 11:13.

Prayer

Lord, I pray that you will cleanse me from my sin and fill me afresh with Your Holy Spirit. I need You to guide and direct me today. Without You, I only have myself to rely on and I am not adequate. Therefore, give me Yourself as I give myself to You today. Amen.

Questions:

1. How much do you rely on your own understanding rather than on God?

2. Do you ask to be filled every day?

3. What could you do or say today that will further an extension of God's Kingdom?

5: Step Out in the Right Direction

Every journey begins with one small step, just as every word and deed begins with one small thought.

Each step that you take will lead towards somewhere or something. Therefore, be aware that just one degree off course as you start, will lead to a wide error in judgement at the end.

One small step in the wrong direction will lead to trouble. All your choices begin with your thoughts. As a man thinks, so he is. Therefore, it is important that you guard your heart and mind. Think about what you are thinking about. Your thoughts can wander into daydreams, wrong desires and selfishness.

It may be that you have been wronged. Your first step could lead to bitterness, the desire to strike back and the need for revenge. Learning to forgive is a hard and unwelcome lesson. It is however the only way to freedom. Take a small step in the right direction and ask for the will to forgive. You will be on the right path.

Guarding your heart - what you love- and your mind - what you think, is vital to your walk with Me. Stay in close touch with Me, allowing Me to correct and guide your path. One small step towards Me will be greeted with open arms and a warm embrace. I love you and want the best for you.

Scripture:

"Be anxious for nothing, but in everything, by prayer and supplication with thanksgiving let your requests be made known to God and the peace of God, which surpasses all understanding, will guard your hearts and minds through Jesus Christ". Philippians 4:6-7.

"Submit yourselves to God. Resist the devil and he will flee from you. Draw near to God and he will draw near to you". James 4:7- 8.

Prayer

Lord, please help me to stay on the path that You have chosen for me. Keep me from turning aside onto wrong paths. May I look to You for guidance rather than leaning on my own understanding. I know Your ways are the best and today I choose You. Amen.

Questions
1. Can you remember a time when you set out on the wrong path?

2. Where did it lead you?

3. Have you a decision to make soon that will affect your future? If so, will you seek God's guidance?

6: You Are of Great Worth

Never for one moment think that you are insignificant. You may not have status, wealth or fame in the world, but you are not of the world. You belong to a different Kingdom. My Kingdom is upside down compared to the world; I do not look on the outside but on the heart.

Consider the widow who put two small coins into the treasury of the temple. She would have felt insignificant, unnoticed by the hierarchy. However, she was not overlooked, I saw what she did, I saw her heart how she gave out of her poverty. To Me, this was significant enough that it is still remembered 2000 years on.

You, too, are very important to Me. I have known you from the foundation of the world. I created you and saw you in your mother's womb. Every part of you is known by Me. When you worship Me you become part of a great orchestra across the earth. As each instrument contributes to a symphony, so you are part of the whole.

I see you when you are struggling, maybe with pain, sickness or depression. Being rejected and put down is also hard to bear. When you refuse to give up and press on you demonstrate your love for Me. At such times I am holding onto you, giving you My strength and power. Therefore, remember always your value and worth to Me, beloved.

Scripture:

"See what great love the father has lavished on us that we should be called the Children of God and that is what we are." 1 John 3:1.

And he looked up and saw the rich putting their gifts into the Treasury and he saw also a certain poor widow putting in two mites. so He said "truly I say to you that this poor widow has put in more than all; for all these out of their abundance have put in offerings for God but out of her poverty she put in all the livelihood that she had." Luke 21:1-4.

Prayer

Lord God, thank You for Your great love for me. Thank You that You know me completely and that I have great worth to You to the extent that You would die for me. Help me to live for You in the light of this amazing truth. Amen.

Questions:

1. Do you truly believe that you are of great worth to God?

2. Or do you sometimes think you must earn His love?

3. What verse or promise could you claim today that will continually remind you of your value?

7: Wait Upon the Lord

Those that "wait upon the Lord shall renew their strength". This was a promise for you given by Isaiah, as you spend time with Me, being still and recognising who I AM, you will receive comfort and strength from My Holy Spirit.

Waiting is often a difficult and frustrating time. You want to see results or answers to prayers come quickly. Waiting is a discipline to be learnt. Children cannot bear to wait, but with maturity comes understanding.

When Moses went up the mountain to receive the Commandments, the Israelites became impatient, demanding something tangible to worship. Thus, the Golden calf was created. What does this represent for you? When things don't happen as you would wish, do you think I have forgotten you? Do you turn back to your old ways, your unregenerate habits and way of living? I told the disciples to wait for the promised Holy Spirit. They were unaware of the amazing power that was to come, power to instigate the age of grace and of the church. They were obedient. They waited prayerfully and expectantly.

As you wait for My return, wait patiently and prayerfully. I always keep My promises. I will return, so look for the signs of My coming and do not turn back to old ways. Do not allow your love for Me to grow cold. Stay close to Me, stand firm and wait, renew your strength and your love for Me and you will be blessed.

Scripture:

But those who wait upon the Lord shall renew their strength; they shall mount up with wings like eagles, they shall run and not be weary, they shall walk and not faint. Isaiah 40:31.

Wait on the Lord; be of good courage and He shall strengthen your heart. Wait, I say on the Lord. Psalm 27:14.

Prayer

Lord, help me to learn patience. I know it is a fruit of the Spirit and that it comes from abiding in the vine. Thank You that I can come into Your presence and spend time with You. I wait for answered prayers and Your return. Amen.

Questions:

1. What causes you to return to your old unregenerate way of thinking?

2. How do you react when you feel your prayers are answered?

3. Do you find that your inner strength is renewed as you spend time with Me?

8: The Problem of Sin

When you have had a drink, do you only wash the outside of the cup? Or when you have eaten, clean only the outside of the bowl? No indeed, you pay more attention to the inside. So it is with your body. You carefully wash with soap and water, but what about the inside, where being clean really counts? Man may look at the outside, but I look within. What goes on inside? Are there ungodly thoughts that can lead to ungodly words and actions? If you say you have no sin you deceive yourself, all have sinned and fall short of My glory.

Therefore, it is vital that you come to Me for cleansing of your soul. Consider your thoughts. Take stock of your words and behaviour and confess anything that grievesMe. Turn away from all wrong that you see in you. I will forgive you and cleanse you from all unrighteousness.

As you mature in your walk with Me you will become more sensitive to My Holy Spirit in you. You will learn to control the unhelpful word before it is spoken, not just regret it afterwards. You will consider your actions and seek My will and guidance. It is better to stay clean then have to deal with the uncleanness after. Spending time with Me in quietness will allow you to grow in love and peace and will lead to following My ways and purposes for you. Remember My plans for you are good and trustworthy because I love you, precious child.

Scripture:

All have sinned and come short of the glory of God. Romans 3 23.

"If we confess our sin he is faithful and just to forgive us our sins and cleanse us from all unrighteousness." 1 John 1:9.

Prayer

Lord, I confess that I sin in word and deed and thoughts. Please put a guard on my lips and a warning in my thoughts to keep me from sin. Thank You that when I confess You are quick to forgive and set me on my feet again. Please fill me with Your Holy Spirit that I become more sensitive to Your ways. Amen.

Questions:

1. What is your weak point, where you are most apt to sin?

2. How quickly do you come to God for forgiveness?

3. How much do you value time spent with God?

9: A Relationship, not a Religion

When you come to Me, you're not coming to a religion but to a relationship. I don't call you to keep a set of rules and regulations. I call you to come into a loving fellowship with Me. My purpose in making you was that you love Me and enjoy a close walk with Me. Some wrongly think of Me as a tyrant, waiting to discipline anyone who steps out of line. This is a lie from the enemy. My way is a way of love which can overcome a multitude of sins.

My way of love caused Me to choose to leave the glory of heaven and come to the earth as a man. The purpose was to be a living sacrifice and pay the price for your sin, in your place, instead of you. Without the shedding of blood there is no forgiveness for sin. Accept this truth in faith and turn from your sin and come to Me. All who receive Me have the right to become Children of God. A small step of faith towards Me results in My coming to you with arms wide to embrace you. I ask you to continue to walk in faith, never thinking that your good works are enough. These good works are like dirty rags compared with the robe of righteousness that faith in Me will give you.

Yes, do the good work ordained for you, but do them in love because you may and not because you must. Our fellowship is most precious to Me as are you. Walk with Me, talk to Me, listen for My voice and you will know the peace and joy that only I can bring.

Scripture:

As many as received him to them he gave the right become the Children of God. John 1:12.

Greater Love has no one than this, than to lay down one's life for his friends. You are my friends if you do whatever I command you. No longer do I call you servants, for a servant does not know what his master is doing; but I have called you friends. John 15:13-15.

Prayer

Thank You Lord, that You made me to be in a relationship with You. You have made me Your child and also Your friend. Keep me from doing things for You as a religion rather than out of love. May our walk together be joyful. Amen.

Questions:

1. What might you do "religiously"?

2. How do you further your relationship with Jesus?

3. Do you spend time listening for His still small voice as well as speaking?

10: Salvation, the Gift of God.

There was once a man called Naaman who was known to be good and honourable, but he was a leper. He was told through a young servant girl that there was someone who could heal him. And so he went to Elisha the prophet who instructed him to dip seven times in the river. Naaman was angry, expecting something far more spectacular. Eventually he was persuaded to do as Elisha said and he was healed of his leprosy.

Everyone who walks this earth, however good and honourable they may be, has a disease, not leprosy but sin. All have sinned and fallen short of My standard for eternal life. However, there is a remedy for this sin. It is through faith in Me, faith in My saving power. I do not ask you to do something spectacular, but I ask you to call on My Name and believe that My death on the cross and the shed blood of that sacrifice can make you clean.

Naaman thought his instruction was too simple a thing and you too may say "surely I need to earn this salvation, do good deeds and give to the poor and work hard?" Such things are honourable, but you cannot gain eternal life through works. This life is a gift from Me, a gift of grace which you can choose to receive or reject. As many as receive Me, believing in Me by faith, I give the right to become Children of God. Come to Me for healing from your "leprosy" and receive My precious gift of life and be washed of any sin so that you may truly walk in My ways and bring My Kingdom to other needy souls.

Scripture:

Now Naaman, commander of the army of the King of Syria, was a great and honourable man in the eyes of his master, because by him the Lord has given victory to Syria. He was also a man of valour, but he was a leper. 2 Kings 5:1.

For by grace you have been saved through faith, and that not of yourselves it is the gift of God not of works lest anyone should boast. Ephesians 2:8-9.

Prayer

Thank You Lord, for Your gift of eternal life which You gave me when I put my faith in You alone. I acknowledge that of myself I can do nothing to earn this life. All that I need for life and godliness comes from You. Today, Lord, I receive all that You have for me. Amen.

Questions:

1. Do you still feel the need to earn your salvation?

2. Do you seek forgiveness and cleansing for your sin on a daily basis?

3. You were made for good deeds. What good thing could you do today?

11: The Plumb Line of God's Word

When I asked the prophet Amos "what do you see?" he replied, "I see a plumb line". A plumb line is a simple device with a small weight tied to a cord. When held up the force of gravity will always cause the line to be straight and true. When constructing a house, the builder must ensure that the walls are vertical and safe. If the walls lean out or in, there is the danger of collapse.

I asked you today to consider your life and how you are building it. Is it straight and true, measured against the plumb line of my word and My will for you? And what of your foundations? Are they built firmly on the rock with a trustworthy cornerstone? If you build your life on the shifting sand of the world and its ways, you are in danger of collapse. The storms of life, trials and tribulations will come. They will buffet you and you will be unable to stand strong.

Look to Me and spend time with Me. Listen to My voice and read My word. Live a life of obedience to all that I ask of you. I will provide you with all you need for godliness and the strength to endure. My ways are the best and My way for you is designed just for you. I have plans and purposes that only you can fulfil, but I need you to follow Me wholeheartedly, seeking the best, the upright and true with a firm foundation. Your destiny is always heavenward, but in the meantime, live a life of love, joy and peace here on earth and you will know the freedom that only I can bring.

Scripture:

The Lord said to me, "Amos, what do you see?" and I said, "a plumb line". Amos 7:8.

No other foundation can anyone lay than that which is laid, which is Jesus Christ. 1 Corinthians 3:11.

Prayer

Lord, give me wisdom, Godly wisdom so that I may build my life on the truth of your words. Help me to be obedient to you in all I do that I may be strong and steadfast. Amen.

Questions:

1. What are you building your life upon?

2. How are you ensuring that you are building well?

3. What Legacy do you hope to leave?

12: The Schemes of Satan

Since the beginning of time, the devil's tactics have remained the same. He comes to tempt with three weapons: the lust of the flesh, the lust of the eyes and the pride of life.

With the lust of the flesh comes the desire to satisfy with sensual pleasures. This can come in the form of gluttony, over-indulgence in food and drink. Also, unholy sexual desires and adulterous thoughts. Any temptation that seeks to gratify the flesh in wrong ways is to be recognised and resisted.

The lust of the eyes is the temptation to have what is not yours, covetousness, the envy of others, thinking the grass is always greener somewhere else. Materialism is a snare that says you will never have enough, never be satisfied with what you have. Be aware of such thoughts and nip them in the bud. The pride of life is the desire to be in control, to be important and admired. A superior attitude says, "I am better than you so listen to what I say and do as I tell you".

All these things are designed by the enemy to keep you from following Me and My ways. He tempted Me in the wilderness after My 40 days of fasting. My weapon against him was "it is written…". The word of God is sharper than a two-edged sword and the devil left me till an opportune time. He had nothing on Me. Resist him at every turn. Use your weapons of prayer and My word. Resist him and he will flee, do not give him a toe hold in your life and you will have a life of love, joy and peace.

Scripture:

For all that is in the world, the lust of the flesh, the lust of the eyes, and the pride of life is not of the Father, but it is of the world. 1 John 2:16.

Then Jesus said to him "away with you Satan! for it is written you shall worship the Lord your God and him only should you serve". Then the devil left him and behold angels came and ministered to him. Matthew 4:10-11.

Prayer

Lord, please help me to recognise the schemes of the enemy who comes to seduce me away from You and Your ways. May I wield my weapons of praise and prayer and resist the lies with "it is written". Amen.

Questions

1. How quick are you to recognise the devil's schemes to bring you down?

2. Do you realise the power that you have in praise, prayer and declaration?

3. Can you finish the sentence… "it is written", with a verse that is meaningful to you and have it ready for times of temptation?

13: Living Water

You live in a dry and barren land spiritually speaking. Many give no thought to Me, their maker. Many have no desire to know Me, and many blaspheme My Name.

As you dwell in this place, you will feel the effects of the antipathy towards me and also the antagonism against Me.

It is vital for you to stand firm in your walk with Me. You need the water of life to flow into you to keep you from the dryness and stagnation around you. Regard Me as an oasis to which you can run for your thirst to be quenched. I have said in my word "if anyone is thirsty let them come to Me and drink… out of your innermost being can flow rivers of living water".
This oasis of My Holy Spirit is available to you night and day. Come to Me every morning to be filled to overflowing so that your day may be blessed and fruitful.

There is so much need in the world: pain and loneliness, fear and despair. I am the answer to the problems. With Me there is life and purpose and freedom from the power and guilt of sin.

Therefore, carry with you the water of life, the good news of My Kingdom. You are salt and light in the world able to make a difference. So be ready to give an answer for the hope that is in you. May My Kingdom come, and My will be done on earth as in heaven.

Scripture

Oh God you are my God; early will I seek You; my soul thirsts for you; my flesh longs for you in a dry and thirsty land where there is no water. Psalm 63:1.

Jesus stood and cried out saying "if anyone thirsts let him come to Me and drink. He who believes in Me as the scripture has said out of his heart will flow rivers of living water". John 7:37,38.

Prayer

Lord, keep me from dryness of soul and stagnation of spirit. Today, please fill me afresh with Your Holy Spirit that I may walk in newness of life. I want to make a difference in this barren land where you are not known or feared. Lord, you are the answer to those in need. Amen.

Questions:

1. Do you ever feel empty and unfulfilled?

2. Where do you find your meaning and purpose in life?

3. How frequently do you ask to be filled with the Holy Spirit?

14: Come To Me with the Little You Have

Bring Me what you have, and see what I will do. You may think you have nothing to give Me, but think again.

A young boy gave Me his loaves and fish and 5000 were fed. Offer Me your little, finance or material things, and I will multiply your offering. The widow in the temple gave two small coins but she won my affirmation and is remembered 2000 years on.

Moses had only his staff in his hand, but used by Me, it became a serpent then a sign of my great power. Give Me your faith and trust and I will do transforming things in your life. Give Me the love of your heart and you will begin to understand and experience the great love I have for you, a love that caused Me to lay down My life for you.

Bring Me your worship and you will be able to turn away from false idols. Those things that tempt and allure you will be seen for what they are in the light of my glory. Worship, given in spirit and in truth, is powerful and life changing.

Come to Me with your prayers, both for yourself and others. Your prayers unloose My hands and bring about those things that are in My will. With these thoughts in mind, bring Me what you have today and you will find that I can do exceedingly abundantly above all that you ask or imagine.

Scripture:

"There is a lad here who has five barley loaves and two small fish, but what are they amongst so many?" John 6:9.

"Assuredly I say to you this poor widow has put in more than all those who have given to the Treasury". Mark 12:43.

Prayer

Lord, I thank You that You can take whatever I offer to You in love and use it to Your glory. You are a creator who can make something from nothing. How much more will You use my offering. Amen.

Questions:

1. What do you have? (think outside the box)

2. You have time, 24-hours a day. Do you give your time?

3. What will you offer to God today that He can multiply for His glory?

15: Jesus - the Rock

When you are feeling overwhelmed, come to Me, the Rock that is higher than you. I am that Rock of Ages, safe and secure. Immovable in the face of the enemy. I do not ask you to take upon yourself the cares of the world. What I ask is that you bring those cares and concerns to Me. Cast them upon Me, for I care for you. I am the God of the impossible, creator and sustainer of all things. I am able to take your worries and set you free. Turn these worries into prayers. This is a powerful weapon in your hand. Remember the singers appointed to march at the head of the army. Through their praise, the enemy was utterly defeated.

Therefore, in the midst of turmoil, praise Me with your whole heart for who I am and what I can do. Give Me thanks, My love endures forever. There is more power in praise than you will ever know.

When your heart is overshadowed with despair, turn to Me and count all that you can think of to give thanks for. An attitude of gratitude will change your negative thinking and begin to lift your spirit. Have at your disposal verses from My word that you can recall at a moment's notice. Saying "it is written" can change your thinking and defeat the enemy. He will flee taking your worries and cares with him. Thus, when you are overwhelmed, come to Me and I will strengthen you and guide you. I will keep your feet from stumbling and hold you steadfast.

Scripture:

When my heart is overwhelmed; lead me to the rock that is higher than I. Psalm 61:2.

"Therefore, humble yourselves under the mighty hand of God, casting all your care upon Him, for He cares for you." 1 Peter 5:6-7.

Prayer

Lord, I ask you to help me to turn quickly to You in times of trial. Sometimes I feel overwhelmed and bogged down with so many things. I know that You can provide me with the strength to get through. You are that Rock beneath my feet. I put my trust in You. Amen.

Questions:

1. Do you go to the Lord quickly in times of trial or as a last resort?

2. Have you learned to turn your worries into prayers?

3. How can you develop an "attitude of gratitude"?

16: One Thing is Needful

When I was in the home of Martha and Mary, Martha complained that Mary was not helping her prepare the food. My reply was "Martha, you are concerned about many things but only one thing is needed".

This is My word for you today, you are concerned about many things, but one thing is needed. That one thing is the same as for Martha, come and sit at My feet and learn of Me. As you do this, the many concerns will be seen from My perspective, and you will receive the strength from Me to deal with them.

You may feel that you have no time to come to Me because you have so much to do. I say to you, "come to Me and your time will be multiplied to you". Put Me first and allow mM to fill you. Ask Me for wisdom and guidance and they will be given to you.

Do not concern yourself with how I deal with others' lives. Do not envy and do not judge. It is for Me to know the hearts of those around you. I am God and you are not. As I said to Peter on the shore "what is that to you, you follow Me".

That is your purpose, to follow Me and My ways to listen for My voice and be obedient. Serve Me with love and loyalty and the burdens and cares of the world will be taken up by Me that you may be set free.

Scripture:

"But one thing is needed, and Mary has chosen that good part which will not be taken away from her". Luke 10:42.

"Come to Me all you who labour and are heavy laden and I will give you rest". Matthew 11:28.

Prayer

Lord, today I choose to sit at Your feet to learn from You and spend precious time with You. I believe that in so doing You will prepare me for the day ahead. May I be filled with Your Holy Spirit to be part of the answer and not part of the problems in the world around me. Amen.

Questions:

1. How important to you is the time you spend with Jesus?

2. How do you measure your priorities?

3. Do you allow external pressures to make your decisions for you?

17: Jesus - Friend of Sinners

Some people treat Me as a "celestial slot machine" coming to Me when they want something. This is offensive to Me. Do you have a friend that you go to only when you want a favour? That friendship has no lasting basis. No, a true friendship is one in which you can share your thoughts, your problems, your day-to-day activities and so on.

So it is with Me. I desire a relationship built on love and friendship. A relationship where you talk to Me daily about your life and all that touches you.

I do not say "ask Me for nothing", not at all. Ask Me according to My will and it shall be done. To know My will is key in your life. As you spend precious time in My presence and reading My word, you get to know Me more and more intimately, to know My character and My heart. Aim to be like Me, your Rabbi. Follow Me, work with Me, talk with Me, look to see where I am at work and put yourself in the way of it.

Always remember that I reserve the very best for you. This includes the best relationship with Me that you can have. You were made by Me for such a relationship, I do not call you a servant but My friend. Therefore, worship Me and enjoy Me forever.

Scripture:

No longer do I call you servants, for a servant does not know what his Master is doing. But I have called you friends. John 15:15.

But we all with unveiled faces are being transformed. 2 Cor 3:18.

Prayer

Lord, it is an amazing privilege that I can spend time with You, the Creator of the universe. May I recognise the value of time spent in close communion with You. I pray that day by day in Your presence you will gradually transform me into all that You would have me be. Amen.

Questions:

1. Do your prayers consist mainly of requests?

2. How much do you value a closer relationship with God?

3. How much time do you devote to this relationship?

18: A Work in Progress

You are work in progress, a masterpiece being created by Me. When you received Me into your life, you were born again by My Holy Spirit, a new creation. However, you still had many rough edges, bad habits, wrong thoughts, unforgiveness and sinful ways.

Dealing with all these things in a single day would have been too overwhelming for you. Sometimes, I do work at a stroke but more often My way is a progression, a process where you are changed little by little. By looking back over your life, you can chart your progress. What do you do now that is good and right that you did not do before your life with Me? So, what have you stopped doing?

If your life were mapped out on a graph there would be ups and downs, but the line would be an upward curve overall. Day by day, as you come to Me, I am teaching you and guiding you. I'm giving you wisdom from above and My Holy Spirit and the strength that you need to live well for Me.

I am able to heal your past hurts and bad memories and set you free from the pain of them. As these thoughts arise, bring them to the cross, allow Me to touch you with My healing love. Do not try to bring them all at once. That is too much. Little by little, I will heal you and transform you. The secret is to come to Me daily for all that you need, and you will gradually be transformed into My masterpiece, ready for heaven in due time.

Scripture:

"I will not drive them out from before you in one year,... little by little I will drive them out." Exodus 23:29-30.

"We are God's masterpiece created in Christ Jesus for good works which he prepared beforehand". Ephesians 2:10.

Prayer

Thank You Lord, that You made me for a purpose. You had plans for my life from the very beginning. Show me, day by day and little by little how I can fulfil what was ordained for me to do. I want to be fruitful and serve You well. Amen.

Questions:

1. Do you truly believe that you are God's masterpiece?

2. What can you do or say today that will bring glory to the name of Jesus?

3. Have you had a bad memory or hurt that you need to bring to the cross today.

19: Jesus the Potter, We Are the Clay

I am the Potter, you are the clay. The clay does not say to the Potter "I want to be a beautiful vase, or make me into a beautiful bowl". It is for the Potter to decide the shape and purpose of his creation.

So, it is with you, I am the Potter who decides the plans and good purposes I have for you. I shape you and mould you as I see best for My Kingdom. It is for you to allow Me to shape you. Do not resist My work in you. As a unique being, I will do something in you that is unlike any other, exactly to My design.

As the Potter, I remove the imperfections from you, the clay. As they surface, little by little I can remove them. However, just as pottery needs to be put into a kiln for firing, so you must go through the fire of difficult times to become the vessel that is valuable to Me and My Kingdom.

I have never said that a life lived with Me would be easy. On the contrary, I said "in this world you will have tribulation". These are the fires that transform you, that give you strength and fortitude. The trials allow you to come alongside others who are suffering similar troubles. You can then minister My love from a heart of true understanding. Therefore, greet your troubles as friends that will shape and bless you. Through it all, I will be able to say, "well done, good and faithful servant".

Scripture:

"But now O Lord, You are our father, we are the clay, and You are our Potter, and we are the work of Your hand." Isaiah 64:8.

"God comforts us in all our tribulation so that we may be able to comfort those who are in any trouble".2 Corinthians 1:4.

Prayer

Lord, I submit myself to You today, knowing that Your plans and purposes for Me are better than my own thoughts and desires. Shape me into the person You designed me to be and use me for Your glory I pray. Amen.

Questions:

1. Will you submit yourself to God today?

2. How have your past trials shaped you?

3. Are you willing to go alongside another to help them with what you have endured?

20: The Way of the World and the Way of Truth

Do not love the world and the things in it. The world and all that it contains will one day pass away, rolled up like a garment and discarded. The love of money is a root of evil. Money itself is not evil, but the wrong desire for more and more. Riches are deceitful, promising much but never satisfying. The more they give, the more they demand. Riches and wealth will never bring true satisfaction; they may bring passing happiness but that soon fades. They may bring a feeling of security, but everything can change in a day and the world as you know it becomes completely different.

Consider the things that will endure for eternity, My word will last forever, people also, and the prayers of the Saints. Put your energy into these things and you will find the security and satisfaction that you have been looking for.

Spend time in My word and regard it as nourishing food for your soul and spirit. Serve others, giving your time and resources to those in need. Remember the poor and do what you can. What you do for the least, you do for Me. Spending time with Me will always be profitable. This is what you were created for. You will receive guidance and strength, wisdom, security, and self-worth. These are what the world unwittingly seeks in all the wrong places. Only I can truly give you all you need for life and godliness. Therefore, come to Me and I will give you the richest of fare.

Scripture:

"Now godliness with contentment is great gain. For we brought nothing into the world, and it is certain we can carry nothing out". 1 Timothy 6:6-7.

"Seek first the kingdom of God and his righteousness and all these things will be added to you". Matthew 6:33.

Prayer

Thank You Lord, that only in You can I find lasting satisfaction and fulfilment. May I not crave the things of the world but look to You for my provision. I thank You Lord that You are enough. Amen.

Questions:

1. Where do you look for your security?

2. How important to you are your finances?

3. What can you do today that will bless someone in need?

21: Persevere

Don't be afraid of failure. If at first you do not succeed in something, don't give up. Consider a baby wanting to walk. He will take one tentative step and fall over. Then he tries again, two steps. His parents encourage him on, "you can do it". I am the parent who encourages you and urges you in your walk with Me, you can do it!

As you spend time with Me, listening as well as speaking, you will find that I put ideas into your head, things that I want you to do. You may say to yourself "I can't do that!" However, if that idea is from Me, I will equip you to do it. Bear in mind, that I may have to instruct you in the way you should go. Persevere in your attempts to do what I ask. Don't give up at the first hurdle. Ask, and keep on asking for guidance, strength and wisdom and you will succeed.

I may also ask you to stop doing something. Do you gossip or speak ill of others? I ask you to stop. The tongue is hard to control and takes some practice. Quickly repent when words come out that you regret. Gradually, My Holy Spirit will make you aware of the words before they leave your mouth. It is for you to keep trying. Don't give up, never stop doing what is right. I am for you. I am a transforming God, and little by little I am teaching you to become the person I made you to be. Look to Me every day and follow My example. Persevere in your endeavours and I will be with you.

Scripture:

"Let us not grow weary in doing good for in due season we shall reap the reward". Galatians 6:9.

"May the God of Peace…… equip you with every good work to do his will". Hebrews 13:20-21.

Prayer

Lord, give me the strength to persevere with the things that You ask of me. Help me to press on when I make mistakes and not give up. Give me Your Holy Spirit today to equip me and show me Your path. Amen.

Questions:

1. What has God asked you to do that you found difficult?

2. Are you someone that gives up easily or do you persevere?

3. Consider what God may be asking of you at this time. Will you obey?

22: I AM the True Vine

I dwell in you and you in Me. Does this seem to be a mystery? Think of a sponge being plunged into a bowl of water. The sponge is in the water and the water is in the sponge. As the sponge is lifted out, the water will eventually flow out. Then the sponge can be filled up again. This is how it is for you. I dwell in you, "Christ in you, your hope of glory" and you live in Me.

Another example of this is seen in My word. Have you read "I am the vine you are the branches" as a branch in Me you are connected to the life-giving flow of My Holy Spirit. Abiding in Me I can provide you with all that you need.

It is vitally important for you to remain in Me. Without the life of the Holy Spirit working through you, you cannot achieve anything of eternal value. Therefore, stay close, connected to Me through your worship, praise, prayer and silence. Be filled every day with My Holy Spirit so that you can be effective in bringing in My Kingdom and ministering to others. I am sufficient for all your needs, enough for you and for you to give away love, time, practical needs and so on.

As you abide, you will live a fruitful life. Love, joy and peace will flow from you and be a blessing to many.

Scripture:

"I am the Vine, you are the branches. He who abides in me and I in him, bears much fruit, without me you can do nothing". John 15:5.

"The fruit of the Holy Spirit is love, joy, peace, long-suffering, kindness, goodness, faithfulness, gentleness, self-control". Galatians 5:22-23.

Prayer

Lord, this is an amazing mystery, that You choose to dwell in me. today I choose to dwell in You also, to abide with You. Help me to become more aware of Your presence day by day, that I may live for You. Amen.

Questions:
1. What does it mean for you to abide in Christ?

2. What steps could you take today to further this amazing privilege?

3. What is your strongest 'fruit'? And which is your weakest of the nine listed in Galatians 5:22? How can you improve it?

23: The Lies of the Enemy

What lie are you listening to today?

The devil hates the fact that you belong to Me and will do all he can to prevent your walk with Me. He whispers lies that are designed for you. He knows how you function and what will affect you most. For some, the lie will be to do with your self-worth and will be that you are a failure, will never do anything worthwhile, useless. When the devil lies, bear in mind that the opposite is true. So if he is saying you are worthless, the fact is that you are very valuable to Me, precious and loved. Loved so much that I chose to die for you. When the enemy comes in with fear, respond with faith. He may say "what if you get sick?" "Can't pay your bills?" "Your children will have an accident?" and many more suggestions. Remember that I am for you and will always be with you. I will strengthen you and uphold you whatever happens. Does he say, "you are ugly and unlovable?" I say, "you are beautiful to Me" and I look not on external things but on the heart.

There may have been times in the past when words were spoken over you that left a wound upon your soul. Recognise these words and remember that hurting people hurt others. Come to Me for healing of these painful memories and allow Me to set you on your feet.

I will restore you and speak truth into your life. I can give you freedom from the pain of the past and bring you into that spacious place that you were designed to do well in.

Scripture:

"Stand fast therefore in the liberty by which Christ has made us free and do not be entangled again with a yoke of bondage". Galatians 5:1.

"There is no truth in the devil……. for he is the father of lies." John 8:44.

Prayer

Lord, help me to discern between Your voice and the lies of the enemy. I know the devil seeks to pull me away from You. May I know Your truth that sets me free and shut my ears to the lies that the enemy speaks. Amen.

Questions:

1. What lie are you listening to today?

2. What is the opposite?

3. What can you do today to resist those lies?

24: Guard Your Heart and Mind

"Be wise as serpents and harmless as doves". This exhortation is given you because you live in a fallen and hostile world. As My children, you are as sheep among wolves. Wolves are intentional in their desire to catch the sheep. So, it is for you. There are many who seek to discredit and deceive those in My Kingdom, the sheep of My pasture.

As you live in the world, you cannot avoid the people of the world, but you can guard yourself from being influenced and deceived by them.

The enemy is always prowling around seeking to cause damage to the Kingdom. Be on the alert for his lies and his ways. Recognise his temptations, not just of the flesh but of the mind and thinking. He would seduce you to an easy life where you avoid the challenge of walking in my footsteps. He will try to deceive you with a false gospel and false doctrines. It is vital for you to be filled with the Holy Spirit, to study My word and know the truth from fiction.

Stand firm on the Rock. Put your roots down into solid ground. Be faithful to Me and the calling which is upon you. Be harmless and innocent in all that you do so that the enemy gets no foothold in your life. Live so that those who seek to harm your faith will have to conclude that they can find nothing to condemn you. Remember, I am with you and will uphold and strengthen you that you may endure to the end.

Scripture:

"I am sending you as sheep among wolves. Be wise as serpents and harmless as doves". Matthew 10:16.

"Be anxious for nothing, but in everything by prayer and supplication let your requests be made known to God and the peace of God which passes all understanding will guard your hearts and minds through Jesus Christ". Philippians 4:6-7.

Prayer

Lord, strengthen me today that I may guard my mind from all unhelpful influences of the world. I know that the enemy seeks to tempt me in many ways. Please fill me with Your Holy presence that there may be no room in me for the ways of the world.

Questions:

1. What are the things that tempt you most?

2. How do you resist these temptations?

3. How did Jesus resist the temptations of the enemy both in the desert and during his life?

25: Those Whom God Chooses

My kingdom is not of this world. It is the reverse of all that most hold in esteem. You see that not many of high standing by human standards or of high birth, not many with the highest intellect are chosen by Me to do My will and work. I choose the foolish things, people of little reputation because I look on the heart and not on the outward appearance. I look for willingness to serve Me, not for gain but through love, those that are eager to be obedient and ready to listen for guidance. I esteem those who have a childlike faith and trust in Me, in and with everything. Consider those people recorded in My word who were chosen, not because of their status but because of their love for Me. Moses was poor at speaking, Gideon, the least in his family and tribe. David was a young shepherd when I saw his heart after Me. Peter was a fisherman, as were others of My disciples. Matthew was a despised tax collector but used to write his gospel of the new covenant.

I chose many women to serve and to save. Those recorded did exploits for Me. Esther saved the nation. Rahab, the harlot, rescued the spies. Mary became the chosen mother for Me. The woman up at the well, despised by the village for her behaviour, was the one to bring salvation to the whole village.

So, I say to you, never consider yourself to be of little value because of your status, intellect or background. I look within for a heart dedicated to Me. I chose you and called you and you are of great worth to Me for who you are, precious and loved.

Scripture:

"Not many wise according to the flesh, not many mighty, not many noble are called." 1 Corinthians 1:26.

The lord said to Samuel "do not look at his appearance, for the Lord does not see as a man sees, for man looks on the outward appearance but the Lord looks at the heart". 1 Samuel 16:7.

Prayer

Thank You Lord, that You have chosen me. I pray that my heart will be to love and serve You. Give me all that I need for true life and godliness, the attributes that You seek and not those of the world. Amen.

Questions:

1. Do you ever feel unworthy of God's love for you?

2. Do you seek to please others rather than God?

3. Will you declare today that you are chosen and loved and equipped for all that God asks of you.

26: Be Faithful in Small Things

Are you a person of integrity, honest in all your ways? Are you faithful in the small things, so that you can be trusted with more?

I see into your heart and know every thought you have. I see you in your solitude and in your interactions with others. I desire truth in the inward parts so that what comes out of you is honest and true.

Guard your mind, because all that you say and do begins in your thinking. Your thoughts are a battleground where the enemy tries to cause as much harm as he can. It is here that you need My strength. Consider your thoughts, and when they are contrary to My ways replace them with what is good and truthful.

As you are faithful to Me in the small things, I will give you greater commissions to accomplish. Therefore, as you sense My nudge for you to act, look to Me for guidance and wisdom however insignificant you may feel the task to be. Remember that great oaks grow from small acorns. One small act may turn out to be of great importance.

As you mature in your walk with Me, My Holy Spirit will whisper things to do or say and things to refrain from doing or saying. Be loyal and faithful to Me and to others so that you are known as trustworthy and honest, someone who can be relied upon. In this way you will grow in the calling I have upon you, and I will empower and guide you.

Scripture:

"He who is faithful in what is least, is faithful also in much, and he who is unjust in what is least is also unjust in much". Luke 16:10.

Behold, you desire truth in the inward parts. And in the inward part you will make Me to know wisdom. Psalm 51:6.

Prayer

Lord, make me sensitive to the prompting of Your Holy Spirit. I do not want to miss out on the opportunities before me. May I be honest and loyal to You and to others and faithful in the small things as well as the greater. Amen.

Questions:

1. Is there anything that God is asking you to do at the moment?

2. What small acts of obedience have you done in the past?

3. What was the result of your obedience?

27: The Joy of Fellowship

Beware the tyranny of the "should", I should do this….I should do that. There are many things in this life that have to be done, and many duties to perform. However, when it comes to your relationship with Me, let it be based on love and joy and never because you feel you "must" please Me. I love you unconditionally and will always love you. It is therefore my heart's desire to spend time in fellowship with you. This is not about religion and religious rules and regulations, it is about taking joy in one another's presence.

Do not confuse your ministry, however big or small you feel it to be, with your relationship with Me. The work that I call you to do is secondary to your walk with Me. Your ministry or your "good works" I have ordained from the foundation of the world. These come from knowing Me, spending time with Me and hearing what I ask you to do. Doing too much or doing what I have not asked of you can lead to burn out of your soul and even resentment. Seek Me always. Know My heart for you and stay in My word. I have made you with special gifts and talents and you are uniquely placed to use them well. As you stay close to Me you will find me guiding you and leading you in the best paths. So, I say again, do not serve Me because you must or should, but out of love and obedience. Doing so will bring peace and satisfaction in your life and together we will bring My Kingdom in.

Scripture:

Whoever keeps His word, truly the love of God is perfected in him. By this we know we are in Him. He who says he abides in him ought himself also to walk just as he walked. 1 John 2:5-6.

You shall love the Lord Your God with all your heart, with all your soul, and with all your mind. Matthew 22:37.

Prayer

Lord, thank You for Your unconditional love. May I cherish our relationship and serve You out of love. Keep me from "religion" and "religious" works done from a sense of duty. Strengthen me today to fulfil Your plans for me. Amen.

Questions:

1. Do you truly believe that you are loved by me unconditionally?

2. What have you done in the past merely because you felt you should?

3. What is God's call upon you now?

28: Keep Yourself from Pollution

Keep yourself from being polluted by the world and its ways. In the beginning, the world was without blemish. When sin came in, everything began to change: Thorns and thistles were a sign of all that was happening.

Through the years, pollution and corruption have gradually increased. The world itself is groaning, waiting for its redemption.

Although you live in a sinful world, strive to keep yourself from the effects that it seeks to have on you. Guard your heart and your mind, your soul, and your spirit. Come to Me daily to be washed and cleansed from all that would cling to you. Seek Me for the wisdom and guidance that only I can provide, to instruct you in the way that you should go. As you are filled in My Holy Spirit you will become sensitive to those things that are harmful-things that separate us. What you see and hear are with you forever, so be careful of those influences that corrupt your mind and soul.

Remember that the enemy always seeks to kill and destroy what is of Me. Resist him at all costs. Study My word for it contains the way of eternal life and all that you need for life and godliness. Set your mind on what is good and pure and honourable. Resist the pull of the sinful world and keep yourself from idols. I will strengthen you in your resolve and show you the best way. Look forward to the day when all pollution, selfishness and greed are gone, and you will dwell with Me forever.

Scripture:

"Finally brethren, whatever things are true, honourable, right, lovely, commendable, if there is any excellence and if anything is worthy of praise, think about these things. Philippians 4:8.

Come out from among them and be separate, says the Lord. Do not touch what is unclean. 2 Corinthians 6:17.

Prayer

Lord, I recognise that there is much that would pollute my mind and spirit. Help me to focus on what is good and right and steer clear of evil. I know I am in a battle, but thank You, Lord, that You fight for me. Amen.

Questions:

1. What things are there that are currently trying to pollute your thinking?

2. Are you sensitive to the prompting of the Holy Spirit when He seeks to guide you?

3. Do you go to the Lord regularly for his cleansing and forgiveness?

29: Jesus - the Light of the World

I am the Light of the World. As you spend time in My presence, I will reveal to you those things that hinder your walk with Me. Nothing can be hidden from Me, and it is to your advantage that any sin or failing is acknowledged so that it can be dealt with.

Therefore, come to Me and confess anything that would grieve My Holy Spirit. I am just and faithful and will forgive and cleanse you of all unrighteousness.

I came to bring freedom. Freedom from the shame and guilt of sin. Freedom from the heavy burden that sin brings. I long to see captives set free, released from the prison that the enemy holds them in. As you confess and repent of anything, big or small, I open the door of your prison so that you can step out into freedom and restoration. As you read My word and as you sit with Me, I am able to bring to your attention those things that need changing., attitudes, unforgiveness harsh words spoken, things left undone and so on can be seen for what they really are, stumbling blocks, spoiling your life. My death on the cross is sufficient for every sin. My forgiveness is always available. As you allow Me into every part of your life, you will grow into the person I designed you to be. You will fulfil the plans and purposes that I have for you, plans that will be important for bringing My Kingdom in.

I am with you and will equip you with all you need to be My ambassador.

Scripture:

"If we confess our sins, he is faithful and just to forgive our sins and cleanse us from all unrighteousness". 1 John 1:9.

"If the Son makes you free, you will be free indeed". John 8:36.

Prayer

Lord, I confess that I do sin in thoughts, words and even deeds. Through Jesus' blood shed on the cross, I ask for Your forgiveness and cleansing today. Show me those things that I need to repent of and make me alert to the Holy Spirit's prompting.

Questions:

1. Is there a sin that you fall into often?

2. Are you quick to judge others or prone to gossip?

3. Will you seek forgiveness and cleansing today?

30: Freedom From Captivity

I am your Redeemer. I came to the earth in order to pay the ransom price for your captivity. You once were held as a slave to sin and selfishness by a hard taskmaster, Satan himself.

Although you did not realise it, you were chained up by this enemy, unable to set yourself free.

I paid the ransom price for your freedom, not with silver and gold but with My own blood, shed on the cross for you. It may seem anathema to you, but without the shedding of blood there can be no forgiveness of sin. This I ordained from the beginning of time.

Now that I have paid the price for your freedom, come to Me in repentance and faith. Come daily for cleansing and forgiveness. Step out of your prison into My marvellous freedom. It was for freedom that I came to set you free.

Do not go back to your old ways of living and thinking. Do not be entangled again with that yoke of slavery. Your former way of behaving was without My guidance and love.

I desire the very best for you. I have plans and purposes for your life. Therefore, choose to live in My freedom every single day, free from the oppression and lies of the enemy. He will never satisfy your inner longing. That can only be met by living close to Me. I designed you, chose you to be part of My kingdom. So, walk in the light and love and freedom that only I can give.

Scripture:

"Without the shedding of blood there is no remission of sin". Hebrews 9:22.

"Standfast therefore in the liberty by which Christ has made us free, and do not be entangled again with a yoke of bondage". Galatians 5:1.

Prayer

Lord God, thank You for paying the price for my freedom from the enemy. I look to You today for the power to live in the good of what You have purchased for me. Fill me now with Your loving Holy Spirit, I pray, Amen.

Questions:

1. In what ways has your life changed as a believer?

2. What do you still struggle with?

3. Are there old habits that you have not left behind?

31: The "Soil" of Your Heart

Today, look to the condition of your heart. Are you hard-hearted, lacking compassion, apt to be judgemental and harsh with your words? Remember that I do not consider outward appearance but look on your heart. I ask you to keep the "soil" of your heart healthy. That is, soft-hearted, ready to be generous in every way and quick to listen rather than quick to speak. Is your heart open to receive from Me? Consider My parable of the sower. It is all about the soil. If your heart is hard like the wayside, the enemy will snatch away what I say, My words will have no effect on you. Past hurts and traumas can be like rocks in your heart; these need to be recognised and healed, rooted out in order for the soil of your heart to be receptive to Me.

The spirit is willing, but the flesh is weak, therefore, do not allow the cares of the world and the deceitfulness of riches prevent you from receiving all that I have for you. The world and its pleasures will never fully satisfy or bring the security you seek.

How do you keep your heart's "soil" healthy? By abiding in Me. That is living in the awareness of my love; spending time in My presence and being obedient to all that I say. Be filled with My Holy Spirit continually and you will bear much fruit, 30, 60 or 100 fold. This is My plan and purpose for you. By living the life designed just for you, you will know security, self-worth and great joy.

Scripture:

"Other seed fell on good ground and yielded a crop that sprang up, increased and produced some 30-fold, some 60-fold and some 100-fold. Mark 4:8.

"May Christ dwell in your hearts through faith; that you, being rooted and grounded in love…….. to know the love of Christ which passes knowledge". Ephesians 3:17 and 19.

Prayer

Lord, soften my heart that I may be receptive to Your love and for all that You have for me. Water the soil of my heart with Your Holy Spirit and guide me that I may bear much fruit for the Kingdom. Amen

Questions:

1. How would you describe the condition of your heart?

2. What steps can you take to make your soil good?

3. Do you allow the things of the world to harden your heart or to soften it?

32: The Power of Words

There is great power in words, for both good and ill. Use the power that you have wisely, for life and not death. Your words can bring comfort and encouragement, inspiration and determination. They can bring healing to a troubled soul and exhortation to press on.

In contrast to the good, words can bring the touch of death, that is guilt and condemnation. They can bring feelings of resentment and bitterness, hatred, and all kinds of evil.

The tongue is a little thing but needs to be tamed as a wild animal needs taming. I am able to give you strength and will guard your lips. Ask and it shall be given you, little by little, My Holy Spirit in you will cause you to be sensitive to what you say and how you say it. Gradually you will learn to hold your words back before they are out. Once out, they cannot be taken in again.

Consider your inner being and repent of all that grieves Me. When you are under pressure, what is inside comes spilling out, anger and unforgiveness are expressed in harsh words.

Therefore, guard your heart and mind. Immerse yourself in My word, given to you at great cost. Treasure it, devour it. It holds the words of eternal life. Use it for the good of many. Declare its words to defeat the enemy and bring down strongholds. My word is the most powerful thing on the earth. It is now unchained for many and is much more powerful than the sword. Use it, declare it, live it, and stand firmly upon it, this precious gift given to you.

Scripture:

"The tongue is a little member and boasts great things". James 3:5.

"Out of the same mouth proceed blessing and cursing; my brother these things ought not to be so." James 3:10.

Prayer

Lord, I confess that I have trouble with my tongue. So often I say things that I then regret. Please help me to be sensitive to the Holy Spirit within that I may guard my words and use them well. Amen.

Questions:

1. How far have you come in taming your tongue?

2. Do you realise the great power of words?

3. Today, will you begin to declare in words the goodness of God? It is powerful!

33: The Multitude of Choices

Without Me you can do nothing of eternal worth. With Me, you can live an abundant life, full of purpose, one that satisfies. With the best will in the world, even your greatest efforts will be as wood, hay and straw if they are done with wrong motives. You can never earn my love or your salvation. My love is freely given and without conditions. Salvation is also a gift to be received with faith and joy.

Every day you will be faced with a multitude of choices, some small, some large. As you sit in My presence, be still and know that I am God. I want the very best for you. I know the end from the beginning, therefore seek My wisdom and ask for My guidance. Take the path that I show you. I am a lamp to your feet and a light for that path.

If you waver, not sure what is best, seek My peace at all times. If you lose the sense of My peace, it is a sign for you to reconsider. My peace is intangible, it passes understanding, but once you experience this peace you will never want to lose it. It is nothing like the peace that is in the world, merely the absence of strife. It is deep and unfathomable, given by Me, but also a fruit grown in you as you abide in Me, the vine.

My plans for you are good, plans to prosper your spirit and cause you to become all that I designed you to be. Following My way will bring those results that are like gold, silver and precious stones, these will last to eternity and will help bring My Kingdom in.

Scripture:

"No other foundation can anyone lay than that which is laid, which is Jesus Christ. Now if anyone builds on that foundation with gold, silver, precious stones, wood, hay, straw, each one's work will become clear". 1 Corinthians 3:11-13.

"Your word is a lamp to my feet and a light to my path". Psalm 119:105.

Prayer

Lord, I realise that I have many choices to make every day. I ask for Your wisdom so that I might make good and right decisions. Guide me on my path that I can follow Your ways and not follow my own understanding. Amen.

Questions:

1. Do you ever make quick decisions that you later reject?

2. How can you train yourself to look to me in your choices?

3. What choices will you face today?

34: Amazing Grace

Today, consider My amazing grace. What great love I have showered upon you that you should be called My child, and that is what you are. You have been born again only through My grace, My unconditional love lavished upon you. It is by grace alone that you have been saved, nothing that you could do would ever be enough for you to gain eternal life. You cannot boast of your salvation, it is a gift from Me to be received humbly and with thanksgiving.

Every day, I pour out My grace upon you in ways that you do not realise. I am with you when you are totally unaware of Me. I seek the best for you with My plans and purposes, unique for you.

Never be of the mind that says, "I can continue in sin, so that grace may abound". Sin separates us. By going against Me, you lose your fellowship with Me, lose My guidance and peace. It is foolishness to treat My grace in this way. If you ever sense the enemy bringing such thoughts, turn away quickly and seek My face.

My grace is enough for every circumstance of your life. Because it comes from My heart of love, you can rest assured that I will provide you with the strength for every situation. Thus, grace is not a one-off event for your salvation, but a daily outpouring of My love towards you. It provides what you need, unearned and often undeserved. Receive My grace for you today and know that beneath you are My everlasting arms.

Scripture:

"My grace is sufficient for you, for my strength is made perfect in weakness". 2 Corinthians 12:9.

"For by grace you have been saved through faith and that not of yourselves: it is the gift of God". Ephesians 2:8.

Prayer

Dear Lord, thank You for Your amazing grace towards me. I know I could never earn my salvation in any way. So, I receive Your grace with great gratitude. Today, make me aware of Your grace being poured upon me. So often I don't realise it. Your love is amazing. Amen.

Questions:

1. Do you still try and earn God's favour by your actions?

2. When did God show you this grace towards you?

3. Will you forward grace to others who don't deserve it?

35: The Fruit of the Spirit

I am the giver of gifts and fruit. The gifts of the Spirit demonstrate My supernatural power and the fruits of the Spirit show My character. The gifts, to be effective, need to come out of a pure heart with good motives. They can then be a powerful signpost pointing to Me.

The fruits of the Spirit develop by abiding in Me the true Vine. Such fruit cannot exist in a vacuum. Just as thankfulness needs a recipient to thank, so love for example, needs someone to show that love to. The fruits of the Spirit are not like the fruit that you eat, like apples which are kept in a bowl, doing nothing, but are for the good of others. Unless expressed, the fruit is without purpose.

When you are born again and become a new creation, love, joy and peace are soon seen. Other fruit, however, takes more time to develop. Patience for example, only comes through adversity. People and circumstances come to try you and therefore patience is hard-won.

Long-suffering too, by its very nature can only develop through suffering, when trials come how do you react? What is inside comes out. Self-control, especially the control of the tongue is a fruit that grows through self-discipline and sensitivity to the voice of My Holy Spirit. It is to be sought diligently as hasty words can harm your witness of Me. Ask Me today to be filled with My Holy Spirit, abide closely in Me and be aware of My guidance. Thus, your character, your fruit, will grow and gradually you'll become the person I designed you to be.

Scripture:

"The fruit of the Spirit is love, joy, peace, long-suffering, kindness goodness, faithfulness, gentleness and self-control". Galatians 5:22.

"If we live in the Spirit, let us also walk in the Spirit". Galatians 5:25.

Prayer

Lord God, help me to abide in You the vine, so that I may bear fruit. I want to be a good ambassador for You in the world. So, may love, joy and peace and so on grow in me day by day, as an expression of Your working in me. Amen.

Questions:

1. Are you abiding in Christ? At home in his presence?

2. Which of the fruits do you find most difficult?

3. Do you appreciate the fruit shown by others? Encourage them.

36: The Pain of Suffering

In the world you will suffer undeserved pain and hurt from others. Hurting people hurt others. It is sad but true. You can be subject to abuse in many forms. When I walked the earth, I too suffered from physical and spiritual pain, from betrayal and slander and all kinds of evil. I understand when you suffer and have compassion for you.

It is vital that you turn to Me at times of hurt and do not allow the desire for revenge or retribution take over your thinking. A grudge held can lead to a bitter root, deep in your soul, which will manifest itself in your words and behaviour.

Holding this attitude within will never harm the person who hurt you, only yourself. Come to Me and ask for the willingness to forgive. Pass over the hurt to Me. Have I not said, "Vengeance is mine, I will repay"?
As an act of your will, begin to forgive, seventy times seven. Forgiveness is powerful, it will set you free. When I was suffering the nails in My hands, I said, "Father, forgive them". The enemy could find no toehold in Me.

As you abide in Me, My power will sustain you. I am able to heal you of the things that you suffer. Emotional and spiritual suffering can be much more painful and crippling than physical pain.

Come to Me my child and I will set you free. You can walk tall in the world knowing that I am for you and that I am with you always.

Scripture:

"Looking carefully lest anyone fall short of the grace of God; lest any root of bitterness springing up cause trouble, and by this many become defiled". Hebrews 12:15.

"Forgive us our trespasses as we forgive those who trespass against us". Matthew 6:12.

Prayer

Lord, please help me to forgive anyone who causes me hurt and pain. Teach me to hand them to You rather than bear a grudge in my heart. I know unforgiveness is like drinking poison. May I become more like You who came to earth that we might know Your forgiveness. Amen.

Questions:

1. Is there anyone who you bear a grudge against?

2. Are you willing, to be willing to forgive?

3. Is there any one from whom you need to seek forgiveness?

37: Walk by Faith, Not by Sight

There will be occasions when My ways surprise and delight you. There will also be times when My ways disappoint or even anger you. Understand that My ways are not your ways nor My thoughts your thoughts. I am God and you are not. I see the end from the beginning and am working out My plans and purposes both in the small and in the big picture. It is when trials and troubles come that you need most faith in Me. Trust Me at all times and know that I am in control. To prepare for the storms of life, build upon Me, your rock, so that you will not be shaken. If you build your life on the shallow ways of the world you will be washed away in the storm.

To have faith and trust in Me, you need to know Me well. This knowledge and closeness, comes through fellowship with Me and from reading My word. Spending time in My presence and taking in My word as food for your spirit, you learn My ways and My thoughts.

In this way you will become rooted and grounded. As your roots go deep into the soil of My love, you draw up your strength and faith in Me. You can become oaks of righteousness, a planting for the display of My splendour.

So, I say to you today, walk by faith and not by sight. Trust Me for today and do not worry about the future, you do not know what it holds. You have today, which is enough for you.

Always remember that in good times and in bad, I am with you and for you and My love for you will never cease or change.

Scripture:

"For my thoughts are not your thoughts nor are your ways my ways, says the Lord. For as the heavens are higher than the earth, so my ways are higher than your ways and my thoughts than your thoughts". Isaiah 55:8-9.

"Whoever hears these sayings of mine and does them I would liken him to a wise man who built his house on the rock". Matthew 7:24.

Prayer

Lord, in the midst of trials and troubles, help me know that You are with me and will carry me through. May I never blame You when things seem to go wrong but remind me that in all things God works together for good for those who know him. Amen.

Questions:

1. Do you get angry with God when your trials come?

2. How do you cope when you are under pressure?
3. What does it mean to you to walk by faith and not by sight?

38: God's Ways and Thoughts

Now you see through a glass darkly. Be prepared to accept that there are things that you will never understand while you are still on this earth. When you come to Me with childlike faith, in My life, My death and My resurrection, you are able to receive Me and receive what I offer, eternal life. This childlike faith is sufficient for you to be born again, a child of the living God.

As a child, you need milk to grow. The simple truth of who I am and those words of scripture that are easy to understand, will be that milk for your spiritual growth.

Human intelligence and cleverness can bring much knowledge, but that alone cannot produce eternal life. Spiritual things are spiritually discerned. Therefore, I ask you to live by faith and not by human sight. In your Christian life, you may have doubts. Doubt is not unbelief, just as temptation is not sin. Unbelief says, "it is impossible". Doubt says, "it's hard to believe, but with God all things are possible". The more you read My word the more your understanding will grow. You can move from the milk to more solid food.

Always ask My Holy Spirit to give you enlightenment. What you read will be stored deep within, so that, at just the right time, it will come to your remembrance. Walk patiently with Me, step-by-step. Little by little you will know and understand more and more. Do not look to your own understanding, but in every way acknowledge Me and I will direct your path.

Scripture:

"For now we see in a mirror, dimly, but then face to face. Now I know in part, but then I shall know just as I am known". 1 Corinthians 13:12.

"Lean not on your own understanding. In all your ways acknowledge him and He will direct your paths". Proverbs 3:5-6.

Prayer

Lord, You are so much greater and higher than me that I can never fully know or understand You or Your thoughts and ways. I praise You because You are God, and I am not. You made me, I am Yours. I trust You to give me enough understanding to become all that You made me to be. Amen.

Questions:

1. Are you happy to say, "I don't understand"?

2. Do you sometimes think you could do better than God?

3. Will you accept God's plans for you today and walk in them?

39: Jesus is the Vine, We are the Branches

The vinedresser works diligently to produce the best possible fruit. He chooses the most suitable soil, the slopes facing the sun and the strong wires to support the branches. He carefully prunes the branches and also prunes away some of the fruit so that only the best can remain.

In My word, you read that I am the vine and you are the branches. My Father is the vinedresser. I desire the best fruit from My children. Since I am no longer present physically in the world, you are My hands, My feet and My voice, My representative to everyone you meet. I have chosen your soil, your place of living. It may seem hard and rocky, but I chose what is right for My plans for you. You have the warmth of My love to cause you to grow and you have My Holy Spirit to give you the support you need to stretch out your branches.

Do not resist My pruning. It is for your good, and the good of my Kingdom. This pruning comes through trials and difficulties. It is painful. I often remove even good things from your life so that the result may be the very best. Do not despise My discipline. Like a good parent, I want only the best for you and it may seem hard at the time but it is always to the end of maturity and the production of the best fruit. By your fruits you are known. Therefore, abide in Me the vine and draw your nourishment from Me. Resist the blight of the enemy and stay close to Me. In this way you will fulfil the plans and purposes I have for you.

Scripture:

"Whom the Lord loves he chastens". Hebrews 12:6.

"I am the vine, you are the branches. He who abides in Me, and I in him, bears much fruit; for without Me you can do nothing". John 15:5.

Prayer

Lord, thank You for this illustration of the vine. I want to stay joined to You as a branch to the stem so that I can receive from You all I need. Thank You for pruning me for my good. May I willingly submit to You, as in love You train me to bear much fruit. Amen.

Questions:

1. What has God called you to be?

2. Are you receiving what you need on a daily basis?

3. How do you cope with discipline?

40: Fighting Giants

Are there giants in your life? Goliaths that come at you, taunting you that you are nothing and your God is not helping you?
Recognise the giants for what they are, the lies of the enemy, so that you may stand up and fight them.

Does the giant of fear intimidate you? It is the enemy's frequently used weapon. Many times you can read in My word the phrases "do not be afraid", or, "fear not". I know your thinking and see your fears. Bring them to Me. Take no thought for the future, that you might suffer ill health or financial problems. You might fear for your safety and security. If you put your faith in Me fully you can fight these fears. Declare that I am good, that I will uphold you. Speak out, "it is written....". With this declaration I defeated the enemy in the wilderness. Does your giant threaten your self-worth and significance? The enemy loves to remind you of cruel words spoken over you. Defy this giant by reminding yourself that because of my great love for you, I died for you. You are of great worth and are wholly significant in My Kingdom.

Because the enemy knows you and hates the Spirit in you, he uses the weapons that will be most effective against you. It is vital therefore that you stay close to Me, filled with My Holy Spirit so that the enemy's lies fall on deaf ears. Stay strong and wield the weapons that I give you, prayer and praise and the power of My word declared.

The giants cannot withstand My power, so fight this good fight of faith and you will prevail.

Scripture:

'Then David said to the philistine, "You come at me with sword and Spear, but I come in the name of the Lord of hosts: the battle is the Lord's"'. 1 Samuel 17:45.

Then David took out a stone and slung it and struck the Philistine in his forehead and he fell on his face to the earth. 1 Samuel 17:49.

Prayer

Lord, I give You thanks that You are for me in my battles. You enable me to overcome the giants in my life. Strengthen me by Your Holy Spirit that together we may walk without fear. I commit myself to You today. Amen.

Questions:

1. What giant are you facing today?

2. Which scripture can you declare against this fear?

3. How can you learn and know the whispers of the enemy?

41: Your Times are in My Hands

Your times are in My hands. When you fully grasp the significance of this fact you will find true peace. This peace passes understanding. It cannot be earned, it is a gift, and a fruit.

I am eternal, no beginning and no end. This is a difficult concept for you to take in because you are bound by time. I made time, 24 hours in a day, to help you live well. Time enough for work, worship, rest and leisure. In this regard, everyone is equal, no one has more time, or less. How you spend your time varies greatly between people. Some rush around at top speed, regarding busyness as a sign of importance while others may waste time in futile pursuits.

To find that peace in Me, come to Me daily for guidance about how to spend your time, what is important and what is not. Many things you are duty bound to do but some things are flexible. What is your priority? How can you spend your time wisely and well? Ask Me, seek My instructions and learn of Me.

During My time on earth, I never hurried but was always right on time. My disciples could not understand why I waited before going to Lazarus, but the delay was for My glory. It demonstrated My power over life and death. My birth and death were at the exact time ordained from the Foundation of the world. Regarding My death, the Pharisees said, "not at the Feast". But the timing was out of their hands. Exactly right. Therefore, trust Me with your life and time. I know the end from the beginning. Leave it to Me and do not be anxious. I am with you always even to the end.

Scripture:

"But as for me, I trust in You O Lord. I say You are my God. My times are in Your hand". Psalm 31:14-15.

"Then Jesus said to them plainly, "Lazarus is dead. And I am glad for your sakes that I was not there, that you may believe". John 11:14-15.

Prayer

Lord, thank You that my times are in Your hands. You know the end from the beginning. I trust You with my life. Help me to use my time wisely and well so that Your Name is upheld in all I do or say. Amen.

Questions:

1. Do you often feel pressurised by others as to how you spend your time?

2. How do you decide what your priorities are?

3. How will you choose to spend your time today?

42: Wisdom From Above

What is the use of wealth and riches in the hands of a fool? They will come to nothing and be wasted. Seek wisdom above all else. Ask and it will be given to you and seeking you will find it.

My desire for you is that you may be wise. Wisdom is more precious than silver or gold. Be wise in My eyes and not in the eyes of the world. Worldly wisdom esteems financial gain, celebrity and material possessions. All of these will fade with time, and it is certain you can take nothing out of the world. Therefore, seek what lasts for eternity.

As you read My word and absorb it as food for your soul and spirit, you will gain wisdom. Consider My life on earth. The religious leaders sought to condemn Me through My words but at every point they were thwarted by My wise answers.

When you are in a difficult situation not knowing which way to turn, speak to Me, request wisdom from Me as to the decisions you should make. By stopping and communing with Me it will give you the opportunity to receive My godly counsel. Godly counsel can also be received from those who know Me well. Be prepared to ask for advice from those you trust, those who have gained wisdom over the years. Solomon pleased Me when he requested wisdom above honour and fortune. Great wisdom was granted to him. However, over the years he became complacent and failed to look to Me and sinned greatly. See to it that you stay close to Me seeking My guidance and wisdom every day. Doing so will protect you from going down the wrong path and keep you on paths of righteousness with Me.

Scripture:

"For the Lord gives wisdom. From his mouth come knowledge and understanding". Proverbs 2:6.

"If any of you lacks wisdom, let him ask of God, who gives to all liberally and without reproach, and it will be given to him". James 1:5

Prayer

Lord, I need Your wisdom every day. I am prone to rush off and make foolish decisions. Help me to seek You and Your wisdom both in small matters and in big. Please give me godly wisdom today. Amen.

Questions:

1. How often do you ask God for wisdom?

2. Would you also seek advice from a trusted friend?

3. What do you need wisdom in and for today?

43: Jesus Came in Order to Die

I chose to leave the courts of heaven and the joy of fellowship, to come to earth as a man. Like Isaiah, I responded to the question "who can I send?" With, "here am I, send Me".

I knew that My path would lead to death on the cross. I knew that a blood sacrifice was necessary to deal with the sin of the world. Nevertheless, I chose that path because of My love for you.

In walking this earth as a man, I had to endure all the pain and hardship common to humanity. I suffered physical, emotional and spiritual anguish. I was despised and rejected, acquainted with grief. I underwent the torture and suffering of flogging and crucifixion, abandonment from My Father, and finally death itself. My face was set as flint to pursue this journey, right from childhood. It was the only way that true fellowship between God and creation could be achieved. Therefore, come to Me with great joy and delight, knowing the measures that I have taken to restore our closeness. Begin to comprehend that great love that I have for you that you may be called a child of God. Through my humanity I can understand your deepest feelings, know what it is like to feel pain and suffering and to resist the temptations of the enemy.

I have sent My Holy Spirit to empower you and fill you, that you may be an overcomer, living with Me and for Me. Therefore, trust Me and choose to serve Me today and for the future, living in close harmony with Me.

Scripture

"Christ Jesus, who being in the form of God, did not consider it robbery to be equal with God, but made himself of no reputation taking the form of a bondservant, and coming in the likeness of men……. humbled Himself and became obedient to the point of death, even the death on the cross". Philippians 2:5-8.

Prayer

Lord, I cannot fully comprehend the enormity of Your leaving Heaven to come to earth as a sacrifice for the sins of the world. I stand in awe of You and worship You for this great love that You demonstrated by Your death. Amen.

Questions:

1. Do you really believe the extent of God's love for you?

2. How can you express your gratitude to the Lord for his love for you?

3. Jesus came to serve. Who can you serve today?

44: The Accuser of the Brethren

The enemy is rightly called the "Accuser of the Brethren". He accuses believers, day and night, looking for an opportune time to bring them down. He loves to remind you of your past sins and failures and knows when you are vulnerable to attack. When I was weak from lack of food, the enemy came to Me in the wilderness. It was an "opportune" time. You are particularly vulnerable during the night hours. If you cannot sleep the enemy is quick to point out where you sinned, trying to fill you with shame and remorse. Watch out for any time that you are Hungry, Angry, Lonely or Tired, HALT! At such times be on your guard for the devil's attacks. He wants you to feel bad, useless and worthless. Consider when an opportune time might be for you. Prepare yourself in advance because these attacks and accusations will come.

I retaliated in the wilderness with words of scripture saying, "it is written". Attack is your best form of defence, so have a weapon of a scripture verse at the ready. Remember especially it is written, "there is therefore now no condemnation for those that are in Christ Jesus". You are set free from the law of sin and death, they no longer have a hold over you. The "therefore", signifies that I have dealt with all your past sins and I now choose to remember them no more.

The accuser could find nothing in Me and so it is with you if you confess your sins and walk according to the Holy Spirit. It is for freedom that I came to set you free, and that includes freedom from accusation.

Scripture:

"There is therefore now no condemnation to those who are in Christ Jesus, who do not walk according to the flesh, but according to the Spirit". Romans 8:1.

Jesus was hungry. Now when the tempter came to Him, he said, "If you are the Son of God………". He answered and said, "It is written, 'Man shall not live by bread alone." Matthew 4:2-4.

Prayer

Lord, make me more aware of the Devil's schemes. I know how he comes to lie and tempt. Keep me close to You so that I can resist him and cause him to flee. Give me words of Scripture that will be a weapon for me. Amen.

Questions:

1. When are you most vulnerable to Satan's attacks?

2. Do you recognise your weaknesses?

3. What verses of scripture have you ready as a weapon against the enemy?

45: Turn the Tables on the Enemy

Your body is a temple for my Holy Spirit. I dwell with you and in you. You are my precious possession, bought at a great price. Not silver or gold but by my shed blood.

As my dwelling place, I ask you to keep that temple holy, that is, set apart from the world, the flesh and the devil. You may consider this an impossible task, but with me all things are possible. When I went into the temple in Jerusalem, I saw the corrupt money changers and my anger was aroused. I made a whip and drove them out, turning over the tables and cleansing that Holy place.

I ask you to come to Me daily for the cleansing that I provide, the forgiveness of confessed sins. Turn the tables on your enemy. Thwart his every attempt to bring you down. What he means for evil I can turn for good. Do not think that you will never succeed. I am with you and My strength is made perfect in your weakness. Therefore, do not give into the devil's schemes. Turn over whatever is on the corrupt table in your heart, unforgiveness, bitterness, rejection, throw them out and allow My presence to fill you. As you walk with Me, you will gradually mature into the person I designed you to be. My presence in you is your hope of Glory.

One day all these struggles will pass, all pain, sin and suffering will be no more, and you will enjoy the delights that are waiting for you in heaven.

Scripture:

"Do you not know that your body is the temple of the Holy Spirit who is in you, whom you have from God, and you are not your own?"1 Corinthians 6:19.

"Then Jesus went into the Temple of God and drove out all those who bought and sold in the temple, and overturned the tables". Matthew 21:12.

Prayer

Lord, I want to be all that You intended for me. Please show me where there is a "table" in my heart that I need to throw over. Strengthen me and show me Your path. Amen.

Questions:

1. Is there anything in your thinking that you need to throw out?

2. What are the schemes that the devil has for you personally?

3. Today, will you resolve to work more closely with your Maker?

46: Don't Be Squeezed into the World's Mould

This world is not your home, you are just passing through on a pilgrimage to your true home, which is in heaven, with Me.

When I called Abraham to leave his home and set out for another country, by faith he left not knowing where I would lead him. You, however, have been called heavenward. You know your destination. Therefore, follow the path set out before you with confidence, knowing that I am with you.

Do not be comfortable with the ways of the world. Do not let it squeeze you into its mould. The ways of the world, with its fleshly desires, are contrary to my ways. In order to be set free from these temptations, come to Me daily so that you may renew your heart and mind. You were designed for better and greater things than the attractions of the world. I made you in My image, made you to follow in My footsteps, learning to be like Me in character and thinking.

I have sent My Holy Spirit into the world to enable you to be the person I planned for you to be from the foundation of the world. Without My Holy Spirit you would find this impossible. With Me, you can achieve My purposes for you. Remember that I have called you to be ambassadors for Me in this alien land. You represent My Kingdom. You speak for Me, on My behalf. I give you all you need to do this, so step out boldly today and I will provide you with strength in body, soul and spirit. Fix your eyes on your homeward goal, a glorious home in heaven after your pilgrimage.

Scripture:

"Do not be conformed to this world, but be transformed by the renewing of your mind". Romans 12:2.

"Beloved, I urge you as aliens and strangers, to abstain from fleshly lusts which wage war against the soul". 1 Peter 2:11.

Prayer

Lord, I know that the ways of the world are tempting. Please help me to choose Your ways rather than be squeezed into a wrong mould. I want to be set apart for You and Your ways. So, I ask for Your Holy Spirit to fill me today. Amen.

Questions:

1. Which worldly thing attracts you away from the Lord?

2. How are you able to resist those things that you know are bad for you?

3. How can you be transformed by the renewing of your mind?

47: Kingdom Currency

The currency of My Kingdom is unlike the currencies of the world. Men strive for earthly wealth, seeing it as a means to meet all their needs. With money you can indeed purchase what you need to live but it will never be enough to supply the deep desires of your heart.

You were made for fellowship with Me, and to this end I say, "come to Me all you who are thirsty, come, buy wine and milk without money and without price". You can bring nothing in your hands that you have not received from Me. All I ask of you is to come with faith. This is the currency of the Kingdom. Trust Me and ask of Me all that you need. My Grace will supply everything for life and godliness.

Because of My great love, I am eager to give. I give life in all its fullness to those who come to Me by faith, abundant life, with purpose and joy.

Therefore today, hunger and thirst for more of My presence, more of My Holy Spirit to strengthen and guide. I will not leave you empty and dissatisfied. I will fill you and overflow you. In this way you will touch others with My love and bear the fruit that comes from Me.

Delight yourself in the richest of fare, the Heavenly manna that only I can give. It comes to you every day for you to gather, wine and milk without money and without cost. I provide for your deepest needs and will satisfy the desires of your heart.

Scripture:

"Then the lord said to Moses "I will rain down bread from heaven for you……..gather enough for that day". Exodus 16:4.

"Ho! Everyone who thirsts, come to the waters; And you who have no money, come, buy and eat". Isaiah 55:1.

Prayer

Lord, I know that You do not give me everything I want, but You provide all that I need. Help me to see that my true needs are not met by worldly currency, but by You. Thank You, that You are enough. Amen.

Questions:

1. Where do you get your security?

2. Do you talk to God about what you need?

3. What will you ask of God today?

48: God's Unconditional Love

My love for you is unconditional. Can you say the same about your love for Me? Does your love for Me wax and wane according to your circumstances? When things seem to go wrong in your life, be it ill health, difficult relationships, financial problems and so on, do you turn away, imagining that I have forsaken you?

My love for you is as constant as the seasons and the returning tide. I will love you come what may. My love is perfect. As God eternal, I do not have imperfections. Therefore, My love can cover a multitude of sins, cast out all fear and bring salvation to mankind.

If you focus on My love for you, it will bring about an increase in your love towards Me. Love cannot be worked up, it is a fruit of the Holy Spirit and therefore dependent on your abiding in Me, the true Vine.

You live in a fallen world, where you will have trials and tribulations. Everyone on the earth is subject to them. How you handle them is what is important. You may rage against Me, blame Me, or even curse Me; or you can come to Me for strength and courage to endure. My peace and presence in the midst of trials is of great worth. I can sustain and keep you close by My side, giving you wisdom and guidance in how to move forward. Try to see your trials as stepping stones rather than stumbling blocks. You can advance and mature in your faith as you put your love and trust in Me and by doing so advance my Kingdom.

Scripture:

"There is no fear in love; but perfect love casts out fear……. We love him because he first loved us". 1 John 4:18-19.

"For God so loved the world that He gave His only begotten Son". John 3:16.

Prayer

Lord, thank You for Your unconditional love. May I too, love You whatever happens in my life. Help me to remember that You are with me in my trials and that You are for me and not against me. Amen.

Questions:

1. How do you react when things go wrong?

2. Does your commitment to God go up and down?

3. Do you blame God when people treat you badly?

49: Commit Your Day to the Lord

Each day is like a fresh clean page for you to write upon. How will it look at the end of the day? Will you be swept along by the pressures of the world, going on automatic pilot?

I ask you to stop for a moment and take stock. Consider your day, its duties, its necessities and its moments of respite. Speak to Me about what lies ahead, but be ready for the unexpected. Only I know what your day really holds. Therefore, invite Me into your thinking, into your plans and into your relationships.

As you spend these moments with Me, bring Me the worship of your heart, the confession of your sins and ask for My Holy spirit to fill you. In this way you will not go into your day unprepared and alone.

As you are able, in the midst of a busy day, find precious times when you can reconnect with Me, maybe to seek guidance in the big things or the small. I know what is best for you and the way that you should take.

Commit your day into My hands, knowing that I am for you and that I love you. Go forward with confidence knowing that I will be with you whatever happens. Do not be afraid of the unexpected or be anxious about what is to come. Seek first My Kingdom and My righteousness. Together, we will walk through this day and at the end, thank Me for the strength and wisdom received.

Scripture

"Trust in the Lord with all your heart, and lean not on your own understanding; in all your ways acknowledge Him, and He shall direct your paths". Proverbs 3:5-6.

Prayer

Lord, I give myself to You today, praying that You will work through me to be a blessing to those I meet. I know that You are with me. Help me to remember You throughout the day and seek Your guidance. Amen.

Questions:

1. How do you start your day?

2. Do you set aside any time to seek God?

3. How do you cope with difficulties and the unexpected?

50: The Gift of Giving

When you give to others, give joyfully and not grudgingly or out of a sense of duty. If your heart is not right, it will be like giving a moth-eaten garment or mouldy bread. I love a cheerful giver, one who gives out of the overflow of the heart not counting the cost but always giving as a result of My prompting or a gratitude for all that you have.

I give and give and give again. Much of what you receive from Me, you take for granted. Consider what you have and not what you do not have. I provide for your needs in practical ways. I also provide for your soul and spirit. Your physical needs are important, but your soul and spirit need provision everyday too.

In considering how to bless others, do not think only of material things, important though they may be. Consider how you can give to benefit another's soul and spirit. Your time is of great value, give it wisely to those who need your input.

I am the Good Shepherd, watching over My sheep, and My lambs. I ask you to look out for those that are in need, especially in My flock and give to them the love and attention as from Me.

As you give joyfully to others, you will receive much more in return, a lapful pressed down and shaken together so that it overflows to give more again. Do not let this truth be the reason that you give but remember that I am no man's debtor and cannot be out~ given. Who can you bless today? Let us together give and give, out of the abundance of all that we have and bring light and joy to others.

Scripture:

"So let each one give as he purposes in his heart, not grudgingly or of necessity, for God loves a cheerful giver". 2 Corinthians 9:7.

"For God so loved the world that He gave……..". John 3:16.

Prayer

Lord, I know that You are a God who loves to give. May I have a heart like Yours, generous and caring. Show me ways to give to others, not just materially, but also for their soul and spirit. Amen.

Questions:

1. Do you consider yourself to be generous?

2. Is your security in your finances or possessions?

3. Who can you give to and bless today; with your time, with what you have or as the Lord prompts you?

51: Keep Yourself from Idols

When you read My word, "Little children, keep yourself from idols", what does it conjure up in your mind? Do you think of a golden calf, or a statue made of wood or stone? An idol you may imagine is for primitive people. However, there is in every person a need to worship. I made mankind for worship and fellowship with Me. Where this is unfulfilled there remains within man a God-shaped blank, a deep cavern that cries out to be filled.

Without Me to fill this space, people choose other things to worship. They may not call it by this name but nevertheless it is so. Having a deep need, some look to celebrities to follow, to seek to know all about their lives. Others imagine that material gain will satisfy but find that they always need more and yet more.

Sadly, there are those that turn to addictive substances that block out the God-given desires and fail to find the one thing that would meet their needs.

Search your heart with the input of My Holy Spirit and ask yourself, "is there anything or anyone that has become an idol in my life?".

Whatever takes priority or sits on the throne for you is an idol. If you find this is the case, repent and ask Me to forgive. I readily do so. Then ask Me that you may be filled with My presence, My love and My Holy Spirit. I will fill that God shaped blank and satisfy your deepest needs. You will know the peace, joy and contentment that is without price, purchased for you on Calvary's cross.

Scripture:

Little children, keep yourselves from idols. 1 John 5:21.

"You shall worship the Lord Your God, and Him only you shall serve." Luke 4:8.

Prayer

Lord, please show me if there is any idol on the throne of my life. I want to serve and worship You only. Fill me with Your Holy Spirit so that my deepest needs are met in You. Amen.

Questions:

1. Will you ask the Lord to show you any idol that you have in your life?

2. What are the longings of your soul?

3. Today will you replace all other gods with the one true living God?

52: The Joy of Heaven

There will come a time when you will be free from all pain and suffering. Every tear will be wiped away and you will know as you are now fully known. You will put on immortality and have no fear or anxiety. You will realise that this new home is what you have been waiting for, the place you were made for, where great delights and surprises abound. Here you will walk by sight, faith fulfilled.

There is, however, a need for patience, it is not yet. What manner of Life should you be living in the meantime? Live on earth as My ambassador, My representative. Do all as if for Me. Allow Me to be the centre of your life. A God centred life will bring you fulfilment and a sense of purpose. Make right choices and decisions with reference to Me, rather than based on your own understanding and desires. Your wants here on earth may be many but your needs are few. These I supply according to my riches in glory. You need My mercy and My grace, without which you could never know Me or My salvation.

Whilst you remain, ask Me daily for My Holy Spirit to feed and sustain you. As you abide in Me, you will produce fruit that will last. Your love, joy, peace and kindness will be a magnet to those you meet. Be a sweet fragrance, so that you will be a light in a dark world, a light that will draw others to Me, like moths to a flame.

Always remember that I am coming back to the earth. Live each day with that in mind, lamp trimmed and ready for the bridegroom's call. Sense the excitement of that day and watch. I am coming soon.

Scripture:

"And God will wipe away every tear from their eyes: there shall be no more death, no sorrow, nor crying. There shall be no more pain, for the former things have passed away." Revelation 21:4.

At midnight the cry rang out: "Here's the bridegroom! Come out to meet Him!" Matthew 25 6

Prayer

Lord, I look forward to my home with You in heaven without pain and suffering. Help me live with that hope whilst walking the rough terrain of the earth. Thank You for giving me this amazing future with You. Amen.

Questions:

1. How can you be heavenly minded while still on the earth?

2. Does this hope spur you on to love and good works?

3. Does your life here reflect your future hope?

53: Beware the Weeds of the Enemy

In My word you can read the parable of the weeds, in which an enemy sows weeds in the midst of the farmer's planting.

This is a warning for you that the enemy is still in the business of planting "weeds". It may take the form of those that come into My church causing disharmony, division, gossip, undermining the work and witness of the body. Test the spirits and be discerning. You know a tree by its fruit, so use the same discernment but with love and care, asking Me for the truth, when it comes to testing the spirits.

The enemy also sows "weeds" into your thinking. Here too, he seeks to bring disharmony and unrest, seeds of doubt and disbelief. As in the natural world, a weed can be dislodged when it first springs up. So, it is in the mind. Consider your thoughts frequently. When you are tired, hungry, unwell and lonely, your mind can be a fertile ground for the enemy's onslaught. Catch all wrong thinking, anything that goes against My word and uproot it quickly.

The lies can be seductive and tempting but will lead to despair. Replace the weeds with healthy plants, those things that are good, worthy and acceptable. Call out to Me for the help that I can provide. Ask for My Holy Spirit and seek out truth. Measure all against the truth found in My word. I am the good farmer who gives the ability for you to produce a healthy crop, 30, 60 or 100 fold even unto old age.

Scripture:

"..the devil……is a liar and the father of lies." John 8:44.

"The Kingdom of Heaven is like a man who sowed good seed in his field, but while men slept, his enemy came and sowed tares among the wheat." Matthew 13:24-25.

Prayer

Lord, keep me alert to the lies of the enemy. Help me to listen to Your truth that I may discern what is true and what is false. Give me a heart after You, to live the truth and speak the truth.

Questions:

1. What are the kind of weeds that the devil seeks to sow in your life?

2. How can you root out these weeds?

3. In what way can you put healthy plants into your thinking today?

54: My Grace is Sufficient

By My grace you have been saved from the clutches of the enemy. Saved, but not by any good deeds that you may have done lest you should boast. Through your faith in Me, you receive the gift of Salvation. My love brought Me from the glories of Heaven to the earth in order that I might die for you, in your place. As a sinless sacrifice, I bought you not with silver and gold but with My own blood.

My grace towards you does not stop at the Cross. It extends to you daily. My grace gives you what you do not deserve. You may consider that all you have you deserve, because of your hard work. Remember, however, that I gave you your abilities, your bodily and mental power to accomplish what you have. Come humbly before Me and thank Me for My grace towards you. I love you and desire the best for you. I am with you and in you, supplying your needs. When you struggle, turn to Me, and know that My grace is sufficient for you. I died that you may live an abundant life. Therefore, seek Me daily and receive My grace poured out for you. Recognise that every good gift comes from above, from the father of light.

Through My grace I give you everything you need for life and godliness. Your past sins are forgiven and as a new creation, you can walk with Me through each day, bringing My love and peace to those you encounter. Yes, My grace is enough for you.

Scripture:

"For by grace you have been saved through faith, and that not of yourselves it is the gift of God, not of works lest anyone should boast." Ephesians 2:8-9.

"My grace is sufficient for you, for My strength is made perfect in weakness." 2 Corinthians 12:9.

Prayer

Lord, thank You for Your amazing grace that you should give me so much that I have done nothing to deserve. Thank You that I am saved by Your grace alone. I could never earn my salvation, so I give You the praise and worship of my heart for such love. Amen.

Questions:

1. Do you ever think that you are good enough to earn your salvation?

2. Do you ever try to bargain with God to get what you want?

3. Will you begin to look for and consider what God's grace does for you every day?

55: Where Are You?

When I made mankind, they were the pinnacle of My creation. I took great delight in walking and talking with them. They were innocent, naked and unashamed. Everything in the garden was lovely.

However, I gave them free will. I wanted love from the heart and not from duty. Through this free will came their choice to disobey Me and to sin. Sadly, at this point, guilt and shame were born and with that came separation from Me. As I walked in the garden, I cried out "where are you?" and this has been My heart cry ever since. "Where are you? I want you back".

The plan of redemption was put in place to rescue the kidnapped, those held in Satan's clutches to keep them from knowing Me.

The perfect unblemished Lamb had to be sacrificed to deal with the sin that separates. Willingly I declared "here I am, send Me."

So it is that all who call on My name by faith can be rescued and brought near to Me. In repentance, each one can be born again as a child of the living God. I still long for that close fellowship with each one of My children. I still call out, "where are you?". Do not allow anything to come between us, between our closeness and fellowship. Quickly repent of anything that might hinder our walk. Draw near to Me and I will draw near to you. When I ask, "where are you?" reply "here I am, speak Lord for your servant is listening" and "here I am, send me".

Scripture:

Adam and his wife hid themselves from the presence of the Lord God among the trees of the garden.
Then the Lord God called to Adam and said to him "where are you?"
Genesis 3:8-9.

The Lord said in a vision, "Ananias." And he said, "Here I am, Lord."
Acts 9:10

Prayer

Lord Jesus, thank You that You went to such lengths to purchase my salvation. Today I choose to say, "Here I am, speak to me Lord". May I be guided and directed by You as I go through this day, knowing that Your plans are good and perfect. Amen.

Questions:

1. Do you ever try to hide from God?

2. Do you have anything in your life that separates you from His fellowship?

3. Will you say today, like Isaiah, "Here I am Lord, send me"?

56: The Love of Many Will Grow Cold

There will be a time when the love of many will grow cold. Those that once loved Me will drift away. Do your utmost so that you will not be amongst their number. How do you keep the flame of your love for Me bright? Firstly, do not try to be a lone believer, saying "I don't need fellowship with others". If you isolate, you will be like a coal taken from the fire, your flame will go out. I made you to be part of a body, therefore meet with others and spur one and another on to love and good deeds.

Secondly, look to your foundations. What are you building your life upon? If your foundations are weak, like the house on sand, when trials and storms come, your faith will not endure. No, build your house, your life, upon Me and my teaching. I Am the Rock. I never change. I am steadfast and true. Look to Me in all things, keeping me at the centre of your life, your reference point. Spend time with Me daily, speaking to Me and also listening. Keep short accounts, so that no sin creeps in. Delve into My word regularly, not just now and again. Study to show yourself a faithful servant. Search out treasures in the word and hold fast to all that you discover. Finally, I would say to you that the fuel for your fire is the Holy Spirit. Without His filling, your flame will grow dim and your lamp will go out. Ask of Me and you will receive, pressed down, shaken together and overflowing to others.

I love you. I am for you. Stay close to Me and keep your love and passion strong and enduring to the end.

Scripture:

"Many false prophets will rise up and deceive many. And because lawlessness will abound, the love of many will grow cold." Matthew 24:11.

"Whoever hears these sayings of Mine, and does them, I will liken him to a wise man who built his house on a rock." Matthew 7:24.

Prayer

Lord God, I do not want my love for You to grow cold. Fill me with Your Holy Spirit today that I will be filled with a passion for You.

Questions:

1. Does your love stay strong in testing times?

2. Do you have a tendency to isolate?

3. How can you fuel your fire for God today?

57: God's Plans for Us.

Come to Me today. I have the words of Eternal Life. Where else can you go? The world will not provide you with the answers you seek. I have had plans for you made from the foundation of the world. You are unique and uniquely placed to bring light and life to your part of the Earth. Just as every cell in the body has its place and function, so you too, as part of a spiritual body, have your role.

Firstly, that role is to come to Me in faith, and worship Me for who I am, and to enjoy fellowship with Me, having your identity in Me. Knowing that you are a child of God, will give you security and self-worth, attributes that are invaluable for your mental health and well-being.

As you draw near to Me, I will draw near to you. Sit in My presence and ask for My Holy Spirit to fill you. Invite Me into your day and allow Me to guide you. With My guidance you will not waste time on fruitless activities, rather you will fulfil all that I had in mind for you, one day at a time. Focus on today and do not stress about tomorrow. Tomorrow is to be lived when it comes!

Ensure that you receive My love for you, so that in turn you may live a life of love. Let everything you do be from a heart of love. Without this you are a clanging symbol, achieving nothing and gaining nothing.

I love a servant heart. I myself came to serve and to be a servant of all. Therefore, serve others in love, in so doing you are also serving Me. Trust in Me today.

Scripture:

"For we are his workmanship, created in Christ Jesus for good works which God prepared beforehand that we should walk in them." Ephesians 2:10.

"Draw near to God and He will draw near to you." James 4:8.

Prayer

Lord, thank You that the plans You have for me far surpass any ideas that I may have. Guide and lead me today that I may be a blessing. Help me to abide in You today. Amen.

Questions:

1. Do you truly believe that God has good plans for you?

2. Where do you go to seek advice?

3. Have you a servant heart? Seek to serve and bless someone today.

58: God Feels Our Pain

I was appointed and anointed to come to earth to share in your humanity, to be like you in every way but without sin. Thus, I knew hunger, tiredness, disappointment, pain and suffering, betrayal, rejection and all sorrow that this world can know.

It can never be said that I don't understand you in the trials and problems that you endure. As I am in you, I suffer with you and as your Great High Priest you can come to Me at any time. My purpose in coming was to bring good news for all, the way of Salvation, to die that you may have life. I came that you may know the great love that I have for you, what more could I do to demonstrate this love than to die that cruel death on your behalf?

I also came and still come to you with compassion and mercy, when you are broken-hearted My heart breaks too. I can bind up that heart with My love and comfort as you pour out all your feelings to Me. There are many who are prisoners. Held captive by chains of fear and anxiety. They are held back from becoming all that I designed them to be. I can break those chains and open the prison doors. Come to Me in complete faith and trust, cast all those fears onto Me. I can take them from you. It is for freedom that I came to set you free. Do not be held in bondage by the enemy. I long to give you a garment of praise instead of a spirit of despair. Receive My spirit and rejoice in Me. I will make you oaks of righteousness, a planting for the display of My splendour. Fulfil your calling, and destiny, as you trust in Me.

Scripture:

"The Lord has anointed Me to preach good tidings to the poor; He has sent Me to heal the broke hearted, to proclaim liberty to the captives, and the opening of the prison to those who are bound." Isaiah 61:1-3.

"For we do not have a high priest who cannot sympathize with our weaknesses, but was in all points tempted as we are, yet without sin." Hebrews 4:15.

Prayer

Lord, thank You that You feel my every pain. You know my inmost thoughts and cares. I come to You today to cast my worries on to You. Set me free from all that would hinder my walk with You. Amen.

Questions:

1. Consider the love that Jesus showed in His death. What more could He do to show His love?

2. Is there anything in your life that holds you as a captive?

3. What will you put onto Jesus today that will set you free?

59: The Power of Praise

There is more power in praise than you will ever know. When Jehoshaphat, king of Judah, was confronted by a vast army he declared to Me, "We have no power against them, we do not know what to do but our eyes are upon You". He set the singers to go before his army to praise Me saying, "Praise the Lord for his mercy endures forever". A simple prayer but the enemy was defeated entirely.

You may not be facing an army, but you will face an enemy, the devil, and all his hosts. In the times of trial and tribulation stand still, remember I am fighting for you. Do not despair, but though it may seem hard, praise Me. Praise Me for who I am and for the fact that I am with you. This is contrary to the way of the world which blames Me for all things that go wrong, forgetting who is the father of lies seeking to kill, steal and destroy.

As you turn to Me, even through gritted teeth, to praise Me, your eyes will be lifted from yourself and the troubles that you are enduring. Rejoice in Me always, not just when things go well. Praising Me is a powerful weapon, a supernatural sword that confounds the enemy. A prayer of praise calls the angels to join the battle. You are never alone, My unseen army is all around. Keep your eyes on Me, "as a maid looks to her mistress". Hold fast to Me, trusting Me. The trials that you endure with perseverance will lead you to greater strength of maturity and character. Therefore, praise Me in all things.

Scripture:

"Rejoice in the Lord always. Again, I will say rejoice! Be anxious for nothing and .... .the peace of God which surpasses all understanding will guard your hearts and minds through Christ Jesus." Philippians 4:4, 6-7.

At midnight Paul and Silas were praying and singing hymns to God, and the other prisoners were listening to them. Acts 16: 25.

Prayer

Thank You Lord, that greater is He that is in me than he that is in the world. I do praise You today because You are a great and mighty God worthy of all my worship. Amen.

Questions:

1. How do you react when things go wrong for you?

2. Do you believe that praise is a powerful weapon?

3. Will you take up this weapon today and see your spirit lifted?

60: True Freedom

Have you been on the receiving end of someone trying to control you? A parent may seek to keep a close control of a child even into adulthood, seeking to shape and mould them without freedom to choose their own path. The result may be that that person then tries to control others and the things around in an ungodly way.

This spirit of control needs to be broken. Each person should be free to make their own choices and decisions. I am able to bring that freedom, ask of Me.

I am a loving God who will not control you, but will guide you in the best path if you ask Me.

Since I am all-knowing, seeing the end from the beginning, I do know what is best for each individual, each one uniquely made by and for Me. It is therefore in your best interests to put Me in the driving seat of your life. I still give you choices every day, but with My guidance they will be good and right.

I gave you free-will from the beginning. Everyone can choose to follow Me or choose to follow their own desires and self-centred ways. You may love Me or ignore Me.

When you choose to put your faith and trust in Me, you will know a freedom that is beyond compare. Together we will navigate your life with purpose and fulfilment. Keep your eyes on the horizon where the glory of Heaven awaits.

Scripture

"In all your ways acknowledge Him and He shall direct your paths." Proverbs 3:6.

"The fruit of the spirit is ..... self-control." Galatians 5:22.

Prayer

Lord, today I hand my life over to You, so that You may guide me and direct my path. I truly believe that Your ways are best and therefore I submit to You. Amen

Questions:

1. What or who is the controlling influence in your life?

2. How much do the ways of the world affect your decisions?

3. Do you truly believe that God's ways are the best and if so, will you submit to him today?

61: Make Room for Me

I came to the earth in humility as a helpless baby, vulnerable and alongside the animals placed in a manger. Sadly, there was no room for us in the inn. Sadly, it is the same today. For many people, there is no room for Me in their lives, they are busy about many things, not giving Me a thought and unaware of their need of a saviour.

Make room for Me today, welcome Me with an open heart that I may fill you, fill you with the power of My love and presence, fill you with all that you need for life and godliness.

Do not allow the world to squeeze you into its mould. You are uniquely made, not meant to follow the crowd unthinkingly but designed to follow the path set out just for you. You are part of My plans and purposes for this world. Do not be daunted by negative thoughts. The enemy will seek to steal, kill and destroy. He lies because he is the father of lies and is full of evil intent.

From being a baby, I grew in wisdom and stature and favour with God and with man. Follow Me and gain wisdom, wisdom from My word and spending time with Me. No longer rely on milk for your growth but choose the meat of My word and grow spiritually. Abide in Me and you will bear fruit, bringing the favour of man as well as of Me. I delight in you and love to see My plans for you unfold. I am with you always even to the end.

Scripture:

"And she brought forth her firstborn son, and wrapped him in swaddling clothes, and laid him in a manger, because there was no room for them in the inn." Luke 2:7.

"For I know the thoughts that I think towards you, says the Lord ...... to give you a future and a hope." Jeremiah 29:11.

Prayer

Lord, today I welcome You into my heart, there is room for You. Fill me with Your Holy Spirit and show me Your plans and purposes for me. Guide and direct me today. Amen.

Questions:

1. Do you truly believe that God has plans and purpose for you?

2. What lie of Satan hinders you from moving forward?

3. Are you enjoying the "meat" of the word or are you still on "milk"?

62: Your Time with God

Will you give Me your best? Or will you give Me that costs you nothing? Have I to make do with the dregs of your day? Maybe five minutes before you sleep when your mind is tired, and you merely pay lip-service to Me. Lip-service is no service. What I look for is heart service, whole-heartedness not half-heartedness.

If you would truly know Me, it is necessary to spend time with Me. Therefore, in the midst of your busy life, carve out a specific time for us to meet and keep it sacred. The enemy will always try to distract you and draw you away. Recognise his tactics and refuse to be sidelined. Everyone has 24-hours in their day. Many spend it wisely, others get swept along by the many pressures of life. Taking time out with Me helps you to prioritise the important things, to seek guidance through prayer and to be still and know that I am God. As you rest in Me, I can fill you with My Holy Spirit, to bless and sustain you.

Do not rob Me of our fellowship. This is what I made you for, having communion together. I love to have your time and attention. It is My great delight and joy. I made you with love, saw you in your mother's womb and watched your life always. Listen for my voice, that still small voice inside you and follow the way that I lead. You will know security, your real identity and great purpose. Test Me in this and see Me open the windows of Heaven.

Scripture:

"Will a man rob God?" Malachi 3:8.

"Go into your room and close the door and pray to your Father". Matthew 6:6.

Prayer

Lord, may my time spent with You bring joy to us both. Help me to make this a priority so that I can get to know You more deeply, and little by little become more like You. Amen.

Questions:

1. How important for you is your time with God?

2. Have you got a time and place set apart for fellowship with God?

3. What tactics does the enemy use to keep you away from God?

63: The God of Love and Truth

I am love and I am the truth. Anything not of love and truth cannot be of Me.

Look for the best in others, rather than the worst. Do not judge until you have walked a mile in their shoes. In love, call out from them the person I designed them to be. Pray and intercede along with the Holy Spirit in you, remembering that I am the God of the impossible. In love encourage and exhort those in need of Me. Love can cover a multitude of sins, and kindness is far more powerful than condemnation.

Love is the first of the fruits of the Holy Spirit. Acts of love and compassion personify Me. You are My voice, My hands and My feet on the earth. Walk worthy of your calling.

Furthermore, seek out truth. I am God and cannot lie. The enemy, Satan, is the father of lies. It is his native language, and he speaks lies to accuse, condemn, confuse, and turn as many as he can from the truth that is found in Me. Ask for discernment so that you can recognise the false. There is much deception in the world, both blatant and subtle. This can cause many to drift from Me and become cold towards Me.

See to it that you remain close to Me. look for the truth that is found in My word. Be true to yourself and true to Me. Honesty truly is the best policy and begins in your own heart. Speak truth in love with care and compassion. Do your uttermost to follow My example, and love and truth will prevail.

Scripture:

"Beloved, let us love one another, for love is of God." 1 John 4:7.

"Judge not that you be not judged. For with what judgement you judge, you will be judged." Matthew 7:1.

Prayer

Lord, empower me to walk in love and truth. Forgive me for judging others when I should not. May I bring love to bear where there is disharmony and truth where there are lies. Amen.

Questions:

1. Do you judge others, even in your heart?

2. Do you allow the lies of Satan to infiltrate your thinking?

3. Where do you need to rethink your attitudes and replace them with love and truth?

64: A New Creation

I have said in My word, "if anyone is in Christ,+ he or she is a new creation the old has gone and the new has come".

When John baptised in the Jordan, he called the people to repent of their old way of life and prepare themselves for My coming.

So too, I ask you to be baptised into Me. Just as a piece of cloth is dipped into the vat of dye and changes its colour, so you, when dipped and immersed in Me, your whole nature is changed. You become new, the old has gone. The old way of life, the old way of thinking and speaking and old behaviours change. You take on My nature as that "new colour". Let no part be tied up, so that "My colour" is lost. I desire a complete change of nature. This may take a while to become manifest in you as the old nature kicks and struggles to have its way.

Persevere on My path, ask to be filled and immersed in My Holy Spirit every day so that the old nature is drowned out.

My Kingdom is not of this world. Worldly thinking and acting are contrary to My plans for you. Therefore, seek to follow Me in faith and trust Me in good times and in bad. My ways and My thoughts are far above your imagining, so let Me be your guide and acknowledge Me in every part of your life.

Together we can do exploits.

Scripture:

"If anyone is in Christ, he is a new creation, old things have passed away, behold, all things have become new." 2 Corinthians 5:17.

"John answered, I indeed baptize you with water but one mightier than I is coming ..... He will baptize you with the Holy Spirit." Luke 3:16.

Prayer

Lord, please show me where my former life seeks to get back in control. Strengthen me daily to resist temptation and instead to persevere on the path marked out for me in my new life. Amen.

Questions:

1. What part of your old life still calls out to you?

2. What do you do to resist it?

3. How is your new life different from your old life?

65: The Peace of God

My peace I give to you. It is not like the peace of the world which is passive, an absence of strife. No, My peace is positive and active. It brings a sense of well-being and contentment. Often it comes as an unexpected gift, in the midst of a trial. It comes with the sense of My presence and of My love for you.

This peace cannot be earned or gained through any endeavour. When you abide and dwell in Me the true Vine, peace is a fruit that comes. You can no more force it than an apple tree can force apples to grow.

As you become conscious of My peace resting in you, you can be also conscious of losing your peace. When this happens, come to Me quickly and allow Me to point out to you where you have gone astray. Repent and turn back to Me. Seek the way you should go or what you need to do. This course of action is a good barometer for guidance. It is also a way for Me to bring discipline to you, because once you have known My peace you will never want to lose it.

As you put your faith and trust in Me you can rest assured with the knowledge that your times are in My hands. I know the end from the beginning, and I can guide and direct you in all your ways. You can know My plans and purposes and be a light in a dark world.

Scripture:

My peace I leave with you, My peace I give to you, not as the world gives do I give to you. Let not your heart be troubled neither let it be afraid. John 14:27.

I trust in You O Lord. I say You are my God. My times are in Your hands. Psalm 31:14-15.

Prayer

Lord God, I thank You for Your peace. It is a precious gift, beyond my understanding. Help me to live by it and value it so that I never stray away from You and lose that amazing gift. Amen.

Questions:

1. Do you have the peace of God in your heart?

2. What do you do if you feel a loss of peace?

3. Will you draw near to God today and allow Him to fill you with His peace?

66: God's Plans are Best

My will for you is good, perfect and acceptable. As My thoughts and ways are so much higher than yours, I know what is best for you. So often you plan and organise your life without thought for Me. Very often these plans are swept away by circumstances leaving you frustrated and annoyed. You do not know what lies ahead therefore let your prayers be prefaced with "not my will but Yours be done".

I came to give you freedom, freedom from anxiety and care. So, give Me your worries. cast all your cares upon Me, knowing that I care for you. Trust Me with your day, one day at a time and with the future.

I am God, enthroned on high. I will be worshipped for who I am, creator, redeemer and Lord of all. It is not for you to demand Me to comply with your wishes. Many of these would be harmful in the long run and I withhold these prayers. If I agreed there would come leanness to your soul.

Trust Me to do what is right. Do not take false responsibility upon yourself. By prayer and supplication let your requests be made known to Me and leave them in My hands. As you lean on Me and My grace and mercy you can experience the peace that passes all understanding. Everything is under My control, so do not fear. When trials and tribulations come, as they will, know that I am with you and can use everything for good. As a loving parent I hold you in the hollow of My hand, you are My precious possession.

Scripture:

Fear not for I am with you.... I will uphold you with My righteous right hand. Isaiah 41:10.

Do not be conformed to this world but be transformed by the renewing of your mind, that you may prove what is that good and acceptable and perfect will of God. Romans 12:2.

Prayer

Thank You Lord, that You know the end from the beginning and that Your ways are always the best. Help me to look to You in all circumstances and put my trust in You at all times. Amen.

Questions:

1. Do you make plans and then ask God to bless them?

2. Do you truly believe that God's will is the best?

3. Will you seek God today for His plans and purposes for you?

67: Beware of False Doctrine

When I was tempted by Satan in the wilderness, I retaliated with the words "it is written". Words of scripture to respond to his attempts to turn Me from My purpose.

However, at his third attempt Satan used scripture himself to try and cause Me to sin. He too said, "it is written" and quoted from a Psalm. Therefore, I say to you, be careful not to snatch a phrase or a sentence out of context for your own ends. Look at the whole counsel of My word for your instruction in life and godliness.

Many have wandered from the truth by extracting a few words and making a false doctrine. Look at who is speaking and what else is said on the subject. Beware of the devil's influence and lies.

For example, you may infer that you can continue in sin because My grace is sufficient. Look further and you will see, "God forbid". When you read that you can, "do all things through Me", does this mean impossible physical feats? Certainly not. The context is of Paul being content with much or with little, being abased, or abounding. He could deal with either.

Thus, it is important for you to read all My word and not just random passages. Ask for My Holy Spirit to guide you. Scripture is given for doctrine, for reproof, for correction, for instruction in righteousness that you may be complete and equipped for every good work. Be diligent therefore and search the scriptures.

Scripture:

Shall we continue in sin that grace may abound? God forbid. Romans 6:1-2.

Then Satan brought Jesus to the pinnacle of the temple and said, "if you are the son of God, throw yourself down, for it is written". Luke 4:9-10.

Prayer

Thank You Lord, for Your precious word. May I be inspired to dig deep into it for the treasures within. Show me Your truth and Your desires for me. Amen.

Questions

1. Do you look mainly for the scriptures that are pleasing to you?

2. Are you also willing to be challenged by the more difficult verses?

3. What is the Lord speaking to you about today?

68: Live for Today

Do not dwell on the past failings and regrets. Focus on today, see it as a gift from Me with, as yet, unseen opportunities. Start your day well, as you mean to go on, with an awareness of My presence. Even in the busyness and turmoil of the day, I am with you. Turn to Me at times of uncertainty and seek My help and wisdom. I am always willing, but love you to ask Me, showing your dependence on Me and trust in Me.

Look for opportunities to encourage, build up and bring comfort and blessing to others. Many are lonely or discouraged and words expressed from a loving heart can be so important.

Do not allow the enemy to steal your time. His lies attempt to turn you from your true path. He may bring doubt and fear, judgementalism and resentment. Resist him with the power of the Holy Spirit in you and defeat him with the sword of My word.

Today is enough for you. do not begin to worry about tomorrow. That will have its own problems to face. No, focus on living well today, doing good where you are able, especially to the household of faith.

Consider that your whole day could be an act of worship to Me. Worship of Me is much more than just prayer and songs, it is a way of life. What you do for others, you do for Me.

Therefore, worship Me with your day and share my love with others.

Scripture:

This is the day that the Lord has made. We will rejoice and be glad in it. Psalm 118:24.

Do not worry about tomorrow for tomorrow will worry about its own things. Matthew 6:34.

Prayer

Thank You Lord, for this new day. May I rejoice and be glad in it. Show me how I should live today. Who can I bless and help with love and encouragement? Please help me to stop worrying about the future and what may or may not happen, but trust You alone. Amen.

Questions

1. How much do you concern yourself with tomorrow and worry about things that may never happen?

2. How do you regard worship? Can it be in the way you live?

3. How can you live well today?

69: Faith with Works

My Kingdom is not merely one of words, but of action, love and joy.
Words alone will not be sufficient for the world to come to Me. Words must be accompanied by deeds. Do not say to someone who is cold and hungry," be warmed and fed", without providing them with the necessities of life.

By all means, preach the Good News in season and out of season but let your words be with kindness and good works.

Be sure to practise what you preach. I am a loving and giving God and you too must love and give. Therefore, be generous and compassionate, not judging others but caring for them.

You are not able to deal with all the needs that you see around. If you try to, you would experience fatigue and burnout. Instead, look to Me and ask Me who you should help and what you should do. In this way your energies will be used to the best advantage. It is useless to cast your pearls before swine, and so you need Me to guide you in the right path. I know the plans I have for you and the works prepared for you from the foundation of the world. Therefore, as you come to Me day by day I can instruct you in the way you should go. Look to My word, it is truly a lamp to your feet and a light for your path. Allow the words to teach you and mature you.

Pray always that My Kingdom may come and My will be done on earth as it is in heaven.

Scripture:

But someone will say, "You have faith and I have works. show me your faith without your works and I will show you my faith by my works". James 2:18.

Be kind and compassionate to one another. Ephesians 4:32.

Prayer

Lord, help me to be aware of Your presence with me today. Show me those in need of love and compassion. Give me a heart like Yours. May my faith and works go hand-in-hand to this needy world. Amen.

Questions:

1. Do you seek to earn God's favour by your good deeds?

2. Do you ask the Lord to guide you on a daily basis?

3. To whom can you demonstrate God's love today?

70: Your Sins are Forgiven

When the paralytic man was let down through the roof, I said "Man, your sins are forgiven. Rise up and walk". When you come to Me in humble repentance and faith, I say again "your sins are forgiven". but I also say to you "rise up and walk".

It is not enough for you to know the freedom of sins forgiven. I ask you to walk, walk in My ways, the ways chosen uniquely for you. Forgiveness was important in this account and remains so, not only My forgiveness but the forgiveness that you have for others who sin against you.

When you harbour a grudge or unforgiveness in your heart, you're not harming the other person as you would wish. No, the harm is being done to you. This anger and resentment poisons your body, soul and spirit. A bitter root grows inside and can only be pulled out by a complete change of heart, total forgiveness. When I forgive, it is complete, and I remember the sin no more.

Therefore, to walk in My way, ask for the will and the power to forgive. As it is a hard thing for you to do, ask Me to strengthen you to be willing. Then make a decision. Allow Me to deal with any retribution and leave it in My hands. Vengeance is mine. I will repay. Then leave the resentment and declare forgiveness in your heart. If necessary, do this seventy times seven times. As you have been forgiven by Me, so you too, forgive others and you will know freedom and peace. It is folly to do otherwise. Forgive as you have been forgiven.

Scripture:

Jesus said to him "man, your sins are forgiven you". Then he said to the man who was paralysed, "I say to you, arise, take up your bed and go to your house". Luke 5:20 and 24.

Looking carefully lest anyone fall short of the grace of God, lest any root of bitterness springing up causes trouble and by it many become defiled. Hebrews 12 15.

Prayer

Lord, I am amazed that You would forgive me and put my sins behind me. Thank You for Your mercy and grace, I deserve nothing, yet You shower me with blessings every day.

Questions:

1. Do you believe that your sins are totally forgiven?

2. To what extent are you able to forgive others?

3. Can you forgive yourself?

71: The Voice of the Shepherd

I am the Good Shepherd who is able to restore your soul. Life brings many trials and tribulations, sickness, sadness, bereavement and so on. All the problems of life are wearisome to your soul, your innermost being. Therefore, when you go through the valleys you need the Comforter, the Holy Spirit, My very presence to sustain you and keep your feet from slipping.

There is always the temptation to rail against Me when things go wrong for you. I take the blame for much of the world's woes. Understand that the enemy is behind the sin and sickness of this present world. He seeks to steal and kill and destroy.

You will never understand My ways while you live on earth, but you can know that I love and care about you. I made you for myself, for a close relationship. When things are seemingly against you and circumstances test you, that is not the time to turn away from Me, but the time to turn towards Me. My loving embrace will hold you, and in My arms, I can restore your soul. I will be with you in your pain to provide the peace and comfort that the world cannot give.

Listen for the voice of the Shepherd. I call you. In good times learn to know My voice so that you can hear Me in times of adversity. One day, all tears, pain and suffering will be wiped away and you will truly know Me, the One who restores your soul.

Scripture:

I am the Good Shepherd. John 10:14.

He leads me beside still waters. He restores my soul. Psalm 23:2-3.

Prayer

Thank You Lord, that You are my Good Shepherd. You restore my soul when I am downcast and in despair. Thank You that You carry me like a lamb when I cannot go on. Help me to distinguish Your voice amongst the many voices that surround me. May I truly follow You. Amen.

Questions:

1. How do you react and to whom do you turn in times of trial?

2. Are you learning to hear the Shepherd's voice?

3. What is your Shepherd saying to you today? (Take time to be still and silent).

72: The Poor in Spirit

Blessed are the poor in spirit. They are the ones who know that of themselves they can do nothing of eternal worth. They recognise their need of Me for everything pertaining to life and godliness.

Others say, "I am rich and in need of nothing". They lay up for themselves treasures on earth becoming puffed up and full of self-importance, loving the acclaim from the world.

To those I say, "you are wretched, naked, poor and blind. You brought nothing into the world and it is certain that you can take nothing out. You leave empty-handed. What will it profit you in the end, if you gain the whole world and lose your soul?"

I look for those who walk humbly before Me having a right appraisal of themselves, not thinking too highly nor yet too lowly. Every good and perfect gift comes down from the Father of light. All good gifts are from Me, your abilities and skills are God-given to be used wisely and well.

Therefore, I ask you to remain with the awareness of reliance on Me for your needs, physical, emotional and spiritual. I can supply all in accordance with My riches in glory. Trust Me in all things, put your faith in Me alone. Thus, as you walk humbly and joyfully with Me you will be blessed. You will know My peace which passes all understanding, My presence with you always and My own unconditional love at all times.

Scripture:

Blessed are the poor in spirit for theirs is the Kingdom of Heaven. Matthew 5:3.

You say I am rich, I have acquired wealth and do not need a thing, but you do not realise that you are pitiful, poor, blind and naked. Revelation 3:17.

Prayer

Lord, I know that in and of myself I can never earn my salvation. You alone can give me what I need for life and godliness. Please fill me with Your Holy Spirit today that I may serve You well and walk in Your ways. Amen.

Questions:

1. How much do you rely on God for your life and your plans?

2. Do you think too highly of yourself or maybe too lowly? (have a right judgement).

3. Will you today seek contentment and peace from God Himself?

73: Self-Pity

Self-pity is a corrosive thing. It eats away at you inside, causing you to be irritable and unpleasant. When things go wrong for you, what is your reaction? Do you immediately say, "why me, what have I done to deserve this?" Wrong question! You live in a fallen world where there are trials and tribulations. A better question might be why not me?

Of course, some trouble will be of your own making. When you make bad choices, behave recklessly and selfishly, when you fall into sin, be assured that things will not end well. At such times "why me?" would be a good question. Search your heart and see where you began to go astray. Repent, turn around and seek forgiveness and get back onto your path. Instead of going your own way, heedless of Me, ask for My instructions and guidance. Follow Me and I will make you all that I intended you to be.
Ask and it shall be given you. That is, ask for My Holy Spirit to fill you and lead you. If you are filled with good, when you are under pressure, squeezed, only good can come out. If you are filled with self-pity and resentment, when you are squeezed that bad fruit will come out.

Therefore, when self-pity comes knocking at your door do not let it in. Look to Me to give you strength to stop. I will sustain you in your need. I have endured great suffering of all kinds, so I can give you the support you need. Come to me and I will give you rest.

Scripture:

These things have I spoken to you, that in Me you may have peace, In the world you will have tribulation, but be of good cheer, I have overcome the world. John 16:33.

The fruit of the spirit is Love, Joy, peace... Galatians 5:22.

Prayer

Forgive me Lord, when I resort to self-pity and think "why me?" In times of testing, help me to look to You for Your strength and guidance. When I am "squeezed" may good words come out!

Questions:

1. When were you last squeezed with a trial?

2. What was your reaction?

3. How can you fill yourself with good and helpful qualities?

74: Aim For Love

Make love your aim. Do everything from a heart of love. Do nothing from selfish ambition or self-seeking. Let your love and gentleness be evident. Love not only those who love you but love those who oppose you and speak ill of you. Pray for them and do not return evil for evil. Remember that a soft answer turns away wrath. Be generous in every way, with your possessions, your finance and especially your time. Give and it will be given to you, pressed down, shaken together and overflowing. But do not give in order to receive. Give even when you know you will get nothing back. I am the one who will reward you.

I gave up the delights of heaven to come to earth. My love for you compelled Me. I willingly gave My life for you, and instead of you because of love. Now, follow My example and live a life of love. Doing all that you can further My Kingdom. Especially love those who are of the household of faith, that the world, might say, "behold how they love one another".

Love is patient and kind. Not envious of others. Not rude or puffed up. Love rejoices in the truth and bears all things. Every quality that you see in Me, try to emulate in your life and the world will be a much better place for it. When you are kind and loving to others it is like a ripple in a lake, reaching out and causing others to follow your example. Therefore, pass love on and see the ripples spread.

Scripture:

Love suffers long and is kind; love does not envy; love does not parade itself, is not puffed up, does not behave rudely, does not seek its own, is not provoked, thinks no evil. 1 Corinthians 13:4-5.

And now abide faith, hope and love, these three, but the greatest of these is love. 1 Corinthians 13:13.

Prayer

Lord, You are love and all You do is through love. Thank You that Your love has bought me, I am Yours. May I follow the way of love today, doing my best to follow Your example. Amen.

Questions:

1. How would you describe your heart?

2. Are you able to love those who hurt you?

3. How can you show love today?

75: Beware of Things That Corrupt

Come to Me, your Rabbi, your teacher. Let Me lead and guide you. There is much in the world that would pollute and try to corrupt you. Be aware of the things that might harm you, things that would pollute your soul and spirit, not just your body.

I am the fountain of life, able to cleanse you, to wash away those pollutants. I can lead you in green pastures and restore your soul. I want you to walk in freedom and joy. Joy is a fruit of My Holy Spirit that comes from abiding in Me, the vine. Joy is a lasting fruit that does not come and go like happiness. Joy is independent of circumstances, like love, and does not disappear in times of trial.

Aim to be like Me. Make it a target and play your part by keeping your eyes fixed on Me, the author of your faith. Do not listen to or watch anything that you know is a pollutant to your soul. Whatever is good and noble and of good report, think on those things.

In My presence and in My word you will be renewed and restored. Drawing close to Me brings you security and self-worth and reading My word will train you in the way you should go. In My light you see light. Carry this into your day. Encourage, exhort and comfort those you encounter and be part of the answer in the world and not part of the problems.

Walk in love and joy, I am with you.

Scripture:

With You is the fountain of life; in Your light we see light. Psalm 36:9.

Whatever things are true, noble, just, lovely, of good report, if there is any virtue, anything praiseworthy, meditate on these things. Philippians 4:8.

Prayer

Lord, help me to steer clear of all that pollutes as far as I am able. May I learn to fill my soul and spirit with good things.

Questions:

1. Think about the things you watch and hear. Are they helpful or unhelpful?

2. Consider what is polluting to you and how can you avoid it?

3. What is the opposite of being polluted by worldly things?

76: Cast Your Cares on Jesus

If you hold a small coin in front of your eye, it seems huge and obscures everything else. When you hold it away from you, in the palm of your hand, you will see it for what it is and in perspective. So it is with your worries. When you hold them close to you, they can seem huge, far bigger than they warrant. Put that worry into My hand and see it more clearly. put it into perspective. It may be that what you are worrying about will never happen. Whatever it may be, I know all about it. I see the end from the beginning and because of My great love for you, I want to take that burden upon Myself. I have said, "cast all your cares upon Me for I care for you".

In time, that particular worry will pale into the past and new cares overtake you. Therefore, learn to give Me your cares as soon as you recognise them. Rehearsing all the, "what ifs" and " how's", will not benefit you but will drag you down. If you trust Me, allow Me to draw near in your distress. Reach out to Me and unburden yourself. I can take it from you and help you to overcome your fears.

Remember that your times are in my hands and that I love you unconditionally and with an everlasting love.

I have made you for freedom - freedom from anxiety and worry. Have faith in me, and together we will handle all that this world throws at you.

Scripture:

Therefore, humble yourselves under the mighty hand of God, that He may exalt you in due time. Casting all your care upon Him, for He cares for you. 1 Peter 5:6-7.

I say You are my God. My times are in Your hands. Psalm 31:4-15.

Prayer

Thank You Lord, that You are willing to carry my burdens. Please help me to cast my cares upon You. May I know Your peace in times of trial and rest in Your arms. Amen.

Questions:

1. Are you someone who constantly worries?

2. Will you begin today to turn these worries into prayers to Me?

3. Which worry will you cast up on Me today?

77: Free Will

I have given you free will. The ability to choose. You may say that I took a big risk. Yes, but it was My desire to give each one the opportunity to choose to love and serve Me or to choose the way of the world and serve other gods.

I take great delight in those who love Me because they may, who serve me out of that love, and not through compulsion.

Each day brings choices. Some are trivial and some are life-changing with many in-between. You have free will, choose today whom you will serve.

I ask you to choose My way because, as a good parent, I know what is best for you, what will give you purpose and fulfilment and the desires of your heart.

Many choices will be difficult. The decision to forgive, for example, may be heart-wrenching. When you have been hurt, then the natural thing is to strike back. However, I call for the supernatural, forgiveness. A choice made, not an emotional response, even to seventy times seven times. I ask you to pray for those who treat you badly and bless them. It is for your benefit, your healing. I will repay. I have not promised you an easy life. In the world you will have tribulation. What I do promise is to be with you in the midst of those trials.

What and who will you choose to follow and do today? Come to Me and receive life. Life and freedom, given from a heart of love.

Scripture :

"........choose for yourselves this day whom you will serve......" Joshua 24:15.

We love Him because He first loved us. 1 John 4:19.

Prayer

Thank You Lord, that You have given me free will. I know that I sometimes make bad choices. Help me to choose to follow You and Your ways and to love You with my whole heart. Amen.

Questions:

1. Which choices you made in the past were bad and which were good?

2. How do you make your decisions?

3. What choices lie before you today and how will you make them?

78: Nehemiah's Task

When Nehemiah was told by Me to rebuild the walls of Jerusalem he began with prayer and fasting. He called the people together and made a strategy to get the work done. Each person had a specific part to play, their own section of the wall to rebuild. Because of the danger from the enemy, some of the people stood guard with weapons at the ready. Some worked with one hand and held a sword in the other. Still others had a trumpet to summon help in time of need. Together, the work was accomplished, the walls were built. Today, I call on you to build My Kingdom, to work diligently together with plans and purposes. Do all with prayerful consideration, seeking My guidance in the way forward for each person.

The adversary, the devil, prowls around to steal, kill and destroy. Therefore, you must arm yourselves with weapons of warfare. My weapons are not those of the world but are spiritual and mighty for bringing down the enemy's strongholds. Have your weapons ready. Pray in the spirit and pray with your mind. Praise Me in all things, it is powerful and turns the tide of evil. Come with thanksgiving in your heart, it will focus your faith and trust in Me and away from your problems. Allow Me to supply all your needs and make My strength perfect in your weakness. Look out for one another. Pray for those on the front line and those who are being persecuted for My Name.

Stand firm with your full armour on and never give in to the schemes of Satan. Remember I am with you always and will uphold you with My righteous right hand.

Scripture:

The weapons of our warfare are not carnal but mighty in God for pulling down strongholds. 2 Corinthians 10:4.

The wall of Jerusalem was completed in 52 days..... my enemies realised that this task had been accomplished by our God. Nehemiah 6:15-16.

Prayer

Lord, You have plans and purposes for me which represent my part of the wall of Your Kingdom. Help me to do my utmost to fulfil the tasks You have for me. May Your Kingdom come, and Your will be done. Amen.

Questions:

1 What is the part that God has asked you to do for His Kingdom?

2. Are you whole-hearted or have you become weary?

3. Do you call upon others to stand with you when the enemy attacks?

79: My Power in You

Open the eyes of your understanding to recognise the greatness of My power extended towards you. It is the same power that caused Me to rise from the dead.

Once you were spiritually dead in your trespasses and sins, but through My great love, I gave life to your mortal body, abundant life for all eternity.

This same power is working in you to enable you to live well in Me. This power transformed My disciples on the day of Pentecost and brought about the birth of My church, My body.

Come to Me daily to receive power for living. Without My empowering, you will function on a worldly level, simply doing what you think best, rather than looking for My best for you.

Never become complacent about the power extended to you. Rather be filled with awe and wonder that I, the Creator all things, should choose to dwell with you and in you. You are indeed a temple for My Holy Spirit. Ask for Me to fill you daily. I will give you all you need for life and godliness. I will give you wisdom and strength to come against the schemes of Satan. He too, wields power but with My power at work in you, you can bring down his strongholds. My power is like dynamite. I am able to do exceedingly abundantly above all you ask or imagine. Have trust and faith in Me. Expect great things of Me. I am for you not against you, so be confident and bold.

Scripture:

...that you may know... what is the exceeding greatness of his power towards us who believe...Ephesians 1:18-19.

The spirit of God, who raised Jesus from the dead, lives in you. and just as he raised Christ Jesus from the dead He will give Life to your mortal bodies by the same Spirit living within you. Romans 8:11.

Prayer

Lord, what an amazing truth, Your Holy Spirit lives in me. That resurrection power is at work in my mortal body! Thank You Lord. Please help me to take it in and live accordingly. Amen.

Questions:

1. Meditate for a moment on God's Holy Spirit in you. How does this affect you?

2. Do you live out of this truth?

3. How will this knowledge affect you today?

80: You are a Child of God

Come to Me that you may know security, self-worth and significance. These are very important attributes for the health and well-being of your body, soul and spirit. The three parts of your makeup need to be in harmony. When you draw near to Me in faith, you receive the security of knowing that I am with you in all things. When you go through the trials of this fallen world, I am right there beside you, to comfort and guide. There is nowhere you can go from My presence. I hold you in the hollow of My hand, but if your foot slips, My everlasting arms are beneath you to set you back on My path.

The enemy lies. He will say you are nothing and nobody, that your work is in vain. But I say to you, I made you, I saw you in your mother's womb and I called you My child. You are of great worth to Me, such that I gave My life to redeem you from the enemy. What more could I do to prove your self-worth than give My life for love of you?

You may not feel important in the eyes of the world, but I have chosen the least to confound the wise and the weak to confound the mighty. Therefore, go in the strength you have in Me, knowing who you are, a child of the living God. Finally, I say, you have great significance. You are important to Me. You are part of My plans and purposes. I have designed you. You are unique. Only you can do the work for Me in your particular corner of the world. Therefore, you have a significant role to play. Hold your head up, My hand under your chin. Look to Me, the author of your faith and know how much I love and esteem you. You belong to Me.

Scripture

See, I have inscribed you on the palms of My hands. Isaiah 49:16.

(God doesn't call the qualified: He qualifies the called)

Prayer
Lord, I Thank You that You give me all I need for life and godliness. You give me self-worth and significance and the knowledge that You hold me securely in Your hands. Amen.

Questions:
1. In what, or in whom, do you place your security?

2. What gives you a sense of self-worth?

3. Do you truly believe that God has a unique plan for you?

81: Suffering

As your great high priest, I walked the earth as fully God but also fully man. I experienced all that it means to be human.
My purpose in coming from the glory of Heaven was to bring salvation to all who would have faith in Me. I understood beforehand that this mission would involve great suffering.

Through that suffering, I know first-hand how hard it is for you to remain obedient to your calling when you find everything going against you. Physical pain, mental anguish, rejection, and persecution are so very difficult to endure. In all of these trials I was tempted to disobey, just as you are. In the Garden of Gethsemane, knowing what was to come, I cried out for another way. However, I declared, "not My will but yours be done". I endured and was obedient to the Father.

In your suffering, know that I am with you and that I sympathise with you. Come to My throne boldly and receive My grace to help you in your time of need.

Therefore, I ask you to learn and experience obedience through the things that cause you to suffer. Do not turn away from Me in anger in difficult times. It is then that you need Me most. Great rewards await those who patiently endure, so receive from Me the equipping that you need. Together, we will see victory and you will hear My, "well done good and faithful servant".

Scripture:

...though He was a son, yet He learnt obedience by the things which He suffered...Hebrews 5:8.

..that I may know Him and the power of His resurrection and The fellowship of His suffering. Philippians 3:10.

Prayer

Lord Jesus, thank You for leaving the glory of heaven to come to earth. How can I thank You enough for enduring such suffering for us. Strengthen me daily to persevere and when suffering comes, to endure knowing that You are with Me. Amen.

Questions:

1. What has been your greatest cause of suffering?

2. How did you cope with it?

3. Do you readily cry out to God in your suffering or take another path?

82: Eat My Word

I have many things to say to you. Some things are music to your ears. Other things may be less appealing or hard to understand.

When you were a baby, you were fed with milk. It was all you could digest. Gradually, you were weaned onto more solid food and eventually meat. This is true in the life of a believer. In the beginning, you need the milk of the word, the things that you can understand and take on board. If you stay only on the milk, you will never grow strong enough to stand, to walk and run your race. You must develop the stomach for stronger "food".

I am the Word made flesh and My written word is life and truth. Develop a hunger for My word, it contains all you need for life and godliness. Delve deeper into it and discover the treasures within. Seek to apply what you learn, and you will dig a solid foundation upon which to build your life. It will challenge you, inform you, correct you when necessary and inspire you to live well.

When you find things difficult to understand, do not be surprised or daunted. My thoughts are higher than your thoughts and some will be too lofty to attain straight away. As you progress in the faith, continue to search the scriptures, "chew" on the "meat" and ask for the Holy Spirit to give you enlightenment.

As you eat My word it will become part of you and when needed, My Holy Spirit can then draw out the things you have discovered. Press on and eat well.

Scripture:

Listen carefully to Me and eat what is good, and you and let your soul delight itself in abundance. Incline your ear and come to Me, Hear and your soul shall live. Isaiah 55:2-3.

Man shall not live by bread alone, but by every word that proceeds from the mouth of God. Matthew 4:4.

Prayer

Thank You Lord, for Your word. I am so grateful for those that died to bring it to us in our language. May I always cherish it and read it carefully, building my foundation and living by its teaching. Amen.

Questions:

1. Do you truly appreciate the power and wealth that is in the Bible?

2. How often and how deeply do you read it?

3. What things have you read that changed your life?

83: Thorns and Thistles

Thorns are mentioned several times in My word. They are symbolic of a curse and of sin. In the beginning, when man chose to rebel against Me, and disobey Me, it resulted in the ground being cursed with thorns and thistles. Thereafter, labour and toil, the sweat of the brow, were needed to survive.

In the parable of the soils, thorns are significant. The seed of the word, when sown among thorns, becomes choked with the cares of the world, the deceitfulness of wealth and the pleasures of this life. Riches are deceitful in that they promise much, such as happiness and fulfilment, but in truth the things of the world, its wealth and pleasures can never bring deep lasting satisfaction. There will always be a blank that can only be filled by knowing Me.

Therefore, be aware of the thorns creeping into your life. The brambles and snares of temptation to seek after other "gods". Cut them out root and branch and be set free. There is also the possibility of Satan causing someone or something to be a, "thorn in your side". Look to Me for the grace that I can give to see you through such hardships and difficulties. I am with you in them to strengthen and guide you.

Finally, consider the crown of thorns, pushed down onto My head at the crucifixion. It represents the sinfulness of mankind so that we needed a Saviour. I am that Redeemer, come to rescue you from the thorns and thistles of the world until you reach your home in glory where there are thorns no more.

Scripture:

Cursed is the ground for your sake. In toil you shall eat of it all the days of your life. Both thorns and thistles it shall bring forth to you. Genesis 3:17-18.

Other seed fell among thorns which grew up and choked the plants. Matthew 13:7.

Prayer

Lord, I know that there are many things in the world that are as thorns to us. Help me to endure the trials with perseverance, knowing that You are with me. Show me how I can make the world a less "thorny" place for others. Amen.

Questions:

1. What are the thorns that you are facing at the moment?

2. How do you personally deal with the thorns of life?

3. Today, consider Jesus suffering that crown of thorns on his head. What is your response?

84: The Peace of God

Seek peace and pursue it. "Seek" and "pursue" are active words, not passive. Once you have experienced My true peace in your heart you will never want to lose it. It is beyond price. My peace is not like the peace of the world. That is largely an absence of strife or war. No, peace is a spiritual state where striving is laid aside and full trust and dependence is upon Me.

As you have received the Holy Spirit, so walk in Him. Peace is a fruit of abiding in the Holy Spirit. I am the vine, and you are the branches, drawing your strength and encouragement from Me. Thus, as you abide, so you will produce fruit, the fruit of peace.

When you are full of worries and cares of the world you will be robbed of your peace. Come to Me with your anxieties. Name them specifically not a general plea. Hand each care to Me and pray that I will guide you. Declutter your mind from all the things swirling around, cast all your cares upon Me for I care for you and My peace which passes all understanding will guard your heart and mind.

As much as lies in you, also live at peace with others. Forgive as I have forgiven you, guard your tongue and exhort and encourage others. Live peaceably. Remember My words, "peace I leave with you, My peace I give to you, not as the world I give to you. let not your heart be troubled neither let it be afraid".

Scripture:

Seek peace and pursue it. Psalm 34:14.

...and the peace of God which passes understanding will guard your heart and mind in Christ Jesus. Philippians 4:7.

Prayer

Lord, thank You for Your gift of peace. It truly passes understanding, we can know peace in the midst of storms! Help me to abide in You Lord that I may bear fruit, especially the fruit of peace.

Questions:

1. Do you have peace in your heart?

2. What do you do when you feel you have lost that peace?

3. Are you truly abiding in the vine that you may bear fruit?

85: Hope

Stand firm in the hope that you have. Hope, the confident expectation that you can rely on Me at all times. When you are in difficulty, look to Me. I am with you and in you. You can trust Me to hold you and sustain you. Since I love you with an everlasting love, do not give into fear, keep your hope in Me.

"Some trust in chariots and horses", is the way of the world, but you have so much more. There is no need for you to rely on worldly wisdom. I am able to guide and strengthen you. Therefore, put your hope in Me. Be confident that I know all things. I know the end from the beginning, nothing is hidden from My eyes. I know who I made you to be, and the race marked out for you alone. Stand firm in this knowledge and do not be afraid.

Put on your full armour, it will guard your heart and mind: your heart with the breastplate of righteousness, and your mind with the helmet of Salvation. Wield the sword of the Spirit, My word, to defeat the arrows of the enemy, the lies that he speaks. Keep that armour on and stand firm in Me, unswayed by the trials you face and the temptation to doubt Me.

Have hope in Me and you will know My peace that passes all understanding. You will have a confident hope of your inheritance, that home in glory kept for you who have kept faith in Me. There is no place for hopelessness and despair in the children of God. Lift up your head and know that there is always hope.

Scripture:

Now hope does not disappoint because the love of God has been poured out in our hearts by the Holy Spirit who was given to us. Romans 5:5.

Some trust in chariots and some in horses but we will remember the Name of the Lord our God. Psalm 20:7.

Prayer

Yes, Lord, my hope is in You. You know what is best and Your ways are perfect. Keep me from looking to worldly ways and help me to trust in You alone. You are my God and I worship You. Amen.

Questions:

1. Where does your hope lie for the future?

2. Have you put on the full armour of God in Ephesians 6: 11-18?

3. When you are down and dejected, how do you move forward?

86: Freedom in Christ

I AM the living Word, eternal, everlasting, without beginning and without end. I have known you from the foundation of the world and made it possible for you to know Me. I came to the earth for that purpose, that in Me you would know the truth and that you would be set free from sin and its power. I am the truth. In Me there is nothing false. I am trustworthy and unchanging, the same yesterday, today and forever. Come to Me, abide in Me. Make Me your dwelling place, just as I come to live in you. Herein lies your hope, of the Glory to be revealed, Me in you and you in Me. As you abide in Me, the Vine, also abide in My word. It is in My word that you come to know the truth that truly sets you free.

There are many ways of being held captive, not just physical. Are you held captive to fear? Fear of death, fear of the future, fear of failure, fear of lack? So many ways for you to be held back by the lies of the enemy. Rest and be assured of My truth and give no place for the lies to take root. Trust Me in all things. Rely on Me for your every need. I am with you and for you. Do not be held captive by the poison of unforgiveness that eats away at your soul. Do not live in the prison of unworthiness, self-hatred, or insignificance.
Come to Me boldly. I open the prison doors, step out, away from all lies and rejoice in the freedom that only I can give. Who the Son sets free ,is free indeed.

Scripture:

Stand fast then in the liberty by which Christ has made us free and do not be entangled again with the yoke of bondage. Galatians 5:1.

He has sent me to bind up the brokenhearted, to proclaim freedom for the captives ...Luke 4:18.

Prayer

Lord, thank You that You came to set me free from the power of Sin and death. help me to recognise where I might become entangled with sinful thoughts and ways and to stay in the freedom that You have given me. Amen.

Questions:

1. What is your point of weakness. Where might you become entangled?

2. How can you stay free from the snares of the enemy?

3. What may cause you to trip up today and how can you avoid it?

87: The Diversity of Creation

I love diversity. Consider My creation, Look at the vast range of animals, from the mighty whale and elephant to a tiny mouse and every size, shape and ability in between. Wonder at the diversity of plant life, massive redwood trees and the beauty of hundreds of different flowers. The colours of the rainbow and the northern lights are a joy to heart and eye.

Humankind is the pinnacle of my creation. Each person has his or her own unique stamp, fingerprint, and DNA. No two people are alike, even twins, and I know each one of you. I made you for Me and in My image. You have a range of emotions, laughter and tears, compassion and mercy.

As I am a creative God, I call you also to be creative, not just in art and literature but be creative in your daily life. Consider how to bless another. Can you make something, give a small gift, spend precious time, remember what would please her or him?

Rejoice in your individuality. Do not let the world squeeze you into its mould. Be renewed daily, and be creative in your thinking. The world calls you to conform to its own ways, but I call you to look to Me and to become more and more like Me.

Follow My ways and My words, be loving and forgiving, not judgemental or critical. Become all that I have made you to be, unique and special, loved by Me and gifted. This is the day that I have made, rejoice and be glad in it.

Scripture:

In the beginning God created the heavens and the earth. Genesis 1:1.

Do not be conformed to this world but be transformed by the renewing of your mind. Romans 12:2.

Prayer

Thank You Lord, for Your amazing creation, for its diversity and beauty. May I notice what You have made and be aware of all the wonder that is around. Thank You too that You made me, unique and to Your design. May I be content with who You made me to be. Amen.

Questions:

1. How much do you notice and appreciate the creation that is around you?

2. Do you accept your uniqueness or strive to be like others?

3. What can you do today that no one else can achieve?

88: Run Your Race

Run with perseverance the race marked out for you. Your race is uniquely for you. No one can run it for you, and you cannot run another's race. It is not a sprint, begun and ended in a day, but more like a cross-country race that will only end when this life is over.

As you step out into the race, lay down anything that would hinder you, any sin that entangles and would trip you up. Confess and be forgiven. Run your race in the freedom that I give.

As you progress, there will be hills to climb and valleys to descend. Often the way is beset with boulders, obstacles to overcome. The enemy seeks to trip you up and take you off course. Be aware of his schemes and resist them till he flees from you.

When you go through the valleys of disappointment, loss, and despair, do not give up. I am with you to comfort and uphold you. Reach out for My hand that together we may get through.

There will be times when you feel as if you are travelling through mud and mire, two steps forward and one step back. This is the time to be resolute and not become weary in doing well. Stand firm in your faith and lift up your eyes. Look to the horizon, the goal of your calling. Fix your eyes upon Me, the author and finisher of your faith. Your goal is your home with Me for eternity. Therefore, run your race and receive the victor's crown and hear My, "well done, good and faithful servant".

Scripture

Let us lay aside every weight and the sin that so easily ensnares us and let us run with endurance the race that is set before us, looking unto Jesus the author and finisher of our faith, who for the joy that was set before Him endured the cross. Hebrews 12:1-2.

Prayer

Thank You Lord, that You endured so much for us. You ran Your race with perseverance. Help me to run my own race with the strength that You provide. May I fix my eyes up on You and upon my goal, eternity with You. Amen.

Questions:

1. What are the obstacles that you are currently facing?

2. What strategy can you have to help you endure?

3. Where will your own race take you today?

89: Wait and Be Still

Be still and know that I am God. The world is a busy and restless place. It calls out to you to act, to be proud of your busyness. You, however, are not of this world but of My Kingdom. I call you to sit quietly in My presence and know that I am your God, your King and your Lord.

Carve out for yourself time in your day when you are able to focus entirely on Me. Let it be free from distractions. Wait, I say, wait on Me. In this way you will renew your mind, your soul and your spirit. Even the young grow tired and weary, but those who wait upon Me shall renew their strength like eagles. These birds soar high and see the world from a lofty perspective. They soar on the thermals and are upheld. You also will gain a new perspective on your problems and your questions. You can relax knowing that beneath you are My everlasting arms.

As you wait, seek My guidance for all that is in your life. Ask Me to fill you with My Holy Spirit and listen to Me. I will guide you with My righteous right hand and I will keep your foot from slipping.

Waiting in My presence is like being filled with fuel for your soul and spirit. You cannot run on empty. You need a daily filling, and this is achieved as you wait upon Me.

I, too, am blessed when you spend this time with Me. I made you for fellowship and intimacy of heart with Me. I take great delight in you, so I say again, "come to me and wait upon me."

Scripture:

Be still and know that I am God. Psalm 46:10.

Those who wait on the Lord shall renew their strength, they shall mount up on wings like eagles. Isaiah 40:31.

Prayer

Lord, I realise that is vitally important for me to spend time with You, to listen, to pray and to worship. As I do so today, please fill me with Your Holy Spirit and guide me in the way that I should go. Amen.

Questions:

1. How important to you is time spent with God?

2. How can you remove distractions?

3. Do you regularly ask to be filled with the Holy Spirit?

90: Worship with Your Whole Heart

The chief calling upon mankind is to worship Me and enjoy Me forever. Broaden your concept of worship. It is so much more than singing, although I love to hear it. Worship Me with your whole life. Make Me central to all you think and do. I will safeguard your steps and keep you from falling into error.

Upon My death, the curtain of the temple was torn from top to bottom, the Holy of Holies opened to all who will come. Therefore, come boldly to the throne of Grace enter My courts with thanksgiving for all your blessings. Name these blessings and you will turn from your anxious thoughts and cares of the world. Take no blessing for granted. Look for the small things that can delight your heart, the song of a bird or a kind word from a friend.

Bring Me your praise. It is a powerful weapon as well as a means of worship. Prayers can bring down strongholds and draw you close to Me. Praise Me for who I am, not just for the things I provide. Consider My many Names revealing My heart and character, Saviour, Healer, Provider and more. Praise Me with your whole heart. Do you realise that when you minister to others, when you help the poor and needy, you are doing it as unto Me? Yes, worship Me as you serve the least, the last and the lost. Never consider your worship with Me as a mere duty or a chore. I want you to know fullness of life, an abundant life, and it begins with being in My presence to worship Me. Therefore, enjoy Me forever.

Scripture

Worship the Lord in the beauty of holiness; tremble before Him, all the earth. Psalm 96:9.

"The chief end of man is to worship God and enjoy Him forever". Westminster catechism.

Prayer

Lord, help me to expand my idea of worship to see that it is a lifestyle and not just a time to sing. May I worship You with my life today by serving others as unto You. Amen.

Questions

1. How would you define worship?

2. Are there other things besides God that you worship?

3. How can you expand your idea of worship to include your way of life today?

91: What is in Your Hand?

I said to Moses, "What is that you have in your hand?" It was a staff, but through My working it became powerful.

What have you in your hand? What gift have I given you that would be powerful for the Kingdom? You may think that you have nothing to offer this hurting world. Think again. I abide in you and have given you My Holy Spirit. This is more powerful than what the world has to offer. The world has nothing that could gain eternal life.

I have given you a unique gift. Designed for who you are and where you are, uniquely placed to bring good news to those around you. Therefore, consider what you are able to do. There are many hurting people, who can you bless? I give the gift of encouragement which can spur another on when they are discouraged.

I love a servant's heart. Where can you serve and whom can you serve? Do it as unto Me not expecting a reward. I also love a cheerful giver. Have you a gift of giving, not just finance but your time, love and concern. Give of yourself from the heart of love. Be generous, not miserly.

See what is "in your hand". Ask of Me and use it wisely and well. Do not bury your gift or lay it aside for another time. Today is the day of salvation and the day to express love to a hurting world. Pick up your "staff" and it will be a powerful instrument in your hand. Be bold.

Scripture:

Then the Lord said to him, "what is that in your hand?" Exodus 4:2.

Every good and perfect gift is from above, coming down from the Father of the Heavenly lights who does not change... James 1:17.

Prayer

Thank You Lord, that You have made us as unique individuals. Show me what I have to offer others, be it big or small. Please equip me to live for You today and to be generous with all I have. Amen.

Questions:

1. Consider what it is you have "in your hand".

2. Do you think that words of kindness, encouragement etc could be your gift?

3. What can you do today that will further the Kingdom of God even in a small way?

92: Be a Peacemaker

Blessed are the peacemakers for they shall be called children of God. There is a big difference between peace-making and peace-keeping. One is active, the other passive.

I call you to be a ministry of reconciliation both between man and God and man and his neighbour. The world is full of strife and dissension but you are not of the world. Such things should have no place in your life.
You can know the peace that only I can give, the peace that passes all understanding. You have been reconciled with the Godhead as you put your faith and trust in My work on the cross, the final sacrifice for sin. Now I call you to reach out to the lost with this ministry of reconciliation that their sins too, may be forgiven and not counted against them.

Seek peace and pursue it. Hold onto your peace by abiding in Me, branch to vine, and bear the fruit of peace. Pursue by keeping short accounts and walking in obedience to Me. Stand firm.

Consider also, how you may seek and pursue peace for the problems that arise between others, especially the brethren. Minister reconciliation with wisdom and compassion as best you can. Ask Me for the Holy Spirit to lead you in the way you should go. I want the world to say of My children, "behold how they love one another". How can this be if there is dissension and disharmony? Bring the oil of My Spirit to troubled waters. Seek out ways to bring peace and love. You will be blessed indeed when you cause true peace to reign in your own life and in those of others.

Scripture:

Blessed are the peacemakers for they shall be called sons of God. Matthew 5:9.

Peace I leave with you, My peace I give to you. John 14:27.

Prayer

Thank You Lord, for Your gift of peace. Peace in my heart that is beyond compare. Help me to maintain this peace within and be a blessing and witness to others. May Your peace be seen in Your body, the church. Amen.

Questions:

1. Do you have the peace of God which passes all understanding?

2. How can you know this peace on a daily basis?

3. In what ways can you bring peace and reconciliation to those believers who are in conflict?

93: The Guidebook for Living Well

I was in the beginning with God and being God. All things were created by the word of My mouth and by Me all things are sustained. I am that God still, the same yesterday, today and forever. I came to the earth, the Word made flesh, to redeem all those who would receive Me by faith. They are made children of God. The words of My mouth are still powerful. I speak things into being. I am the Creator God.

In addition to giving you Myself, I give you My written Word. In it you will find the words of life. Where else can you go for eternal life? Not only do I give you this life, but through My Word, I show you how to live that life. It is a map for your path. A guidebook for living with purpose and fulfilment. When you are in despair or distress, My Word can comfort, exhort and encourage you to press on, knowing that I care and that I am with you.

There will be times when reading My Word, a phrase will seem to jump out from the page and speak directly to your heart, to your circumstances. This is My rhema word, my "now" word. It is given to bring light to your feet and a lamp to your path. When you are born again you need the milk of My Word. However, as you grow you need to move to solid food, the meat so that you mature. How can you grow up if you do not feed on the Bread of Life.? Read My word daily and act on what you learn, by doing so you will build upon the Rock. When the storms of life come, you will stand firm. Yes, stand firm and having done all STAND, on My Word.

Scripture:

In the beginning was the Word, and the Word was with God, and the Word was God. John 1:1.

All scripture is God-breathed and is useful for teaching, rebuking, correcting and training in righteousness, so that the man of God may be thoroughly equipped for every good work. 2 Timothy 3:16-17.

Prayer

Thank You Lord, that You are the Word made flesh, come to give us life. Thank You that You have made yourself known through Your written word. By it we have the knowledge of life and how to live. May I cherish Your word every day. Amen.

Questions:

1. How important to you is the word of God, the Bible?

2. Do you set aside time to read it regularly?

3. Do you regard it as the template for your life?

94: Walk Humbly with Me

Blessed are the poor in spirit for theirs is the Kingdom of Heaven. You are blessed indeed when you recognise that in and of yourself you can achieve nothing of eternal worth. Come to Me humbly and with a contrite heart and allow Me to cleanse you and fill you with My presence. I resist those who are proud, who consider themselves rich and in need of nothing. But I give Grace to the humble. Remember that I created you and gave you your abilities and gifts. All that you had and are comes from Me, all good and perfect gifts from the Father of light.

Allow Me to be like the potter. Be the clay and My hands that I may shape you into all that I planned you to become. I know the plans and purposes I have for you. My will is both acceptable and perfect. Therefore, submit to Me in all your ways and you will be fulfilled and be blessed.

I want you to know more than happiness which changes with your circumstances. I want you to have the deep joy and perfect peace that comes from knowing Me and walking with Me in the paths of righteousness. This heavenly joy and peace is beyond compare. It is the fruit of living an abundant life, set free from the power of sin and death.

I made you to know My blessing and to be a blessing. Carry My presence wherever you go: change the atmosphere with My love. You are blessed indeed when you know your identity as a child of God, looking to Me for your needs and for your filling.

Scripture:

Blessed are the poor in spirit, for theirs is the kingdom of heaven. Matthew 5:3.

God resists the proud. but gives Grace to the humble. James 4:6.

Prayer

Lord, may I walk humbly in Your presence today. I know that You have made me, and You know what is best. Deliver me from any pride and self-seeking. I trust You with my life and recognise that my times are in Your hands. Amen.

Questions:

1. Do you have false pride in any form?

2. Do you consider humility a weakness?

3. How can you experience the deep joy and peace that only God can provide?

95: You are Body, Soul, and Spirit

You take care of your body. You wash, feed and clothe it. Take care of your soul and spirit also, your body is temporal and will pass away, but your soul and spirit are for eternity. How much more should you care for them.

You have been baptised into new life. It is a powerful witness to the world and the enemy. Coming to Me as Lord, your sins were washed away in those waters of baptism. Be cleansed daily by confessing all wrongs and receive My forgiveness. You have been saved through the washing of regeneration and renewing of the Holy Spirit who has been poured out abundantly. As you desire good, healthy food for your body, feed your soul and spirit with the good food of My word, milk when you are young in the faith and going on to meat as you mature. Take in this spiritual food daily to sustain you and hold you steadfast. You cannot run a race without nourishment. Therefore, labour for the food which endures to everlasting life which I will give you. I am the Bread of life. He who comes to Me and believes in Me shall never hunger and thirst. As you physically clothe your body, so clothe yourself with spiritual clothing. When you put your faith and trust in Me, I clothe you with a robe of righteousness. It is not given because of your righteousness but I cover you with mine. Be aware of this tremendous privilege and walk well. Put on your new self, the old has gone. Finally, put on the armour that I provide, that you may stand firm against the schemes of Satan. be strong in My strength and be renewed.

Scripture:

...according to his mercy he saved us, through the washing of regeneration and renewingofy the Holy Spirit. Titus 3:5.

My soul will be joyful in my God, for He has clothed me with the garments of salvation. He has covered me with the robe of righteousness. Isaiah 61:10.

Prayer

Thank You Lord, that You came for me, body, soul and spirit. May I nurture my whole being in ways that are good and helpful. May I feed on Your word and be aware of my robes of righteousness that You purchased for me. Show me Your paths and teach me Your ways. Amen.

Questions:

1. Have you been baptised in water and in the Holy Spirit?

2. Do you regard feeding on God's word as important as your daily bread?

3. Consider the "armour of God" in Ephesians 6. Are you wearing each part?

96: Your Past

Are you ploughing a straight furrow? If you repeatedly look back, you will find it impossible. There are two ways that you can look back to your past. The first is similar to the wanderers in the wilderness looking back to the days of bitter slavery as if they were good days, where they enjoyed garlic and leeks. I delivered them from slavery in a dramatic way and yet they refused to believe that I could bring them safely to the promised land. Do not fall into the trap of thinking that your days before your salvation were better than the freedom you now have. You have been set free from the power of sin and death, rejoice in your life. Look towards your promised land, the ultimate home in glory.

Alternatively, you may look back to your former life with such regret that you cannot fully enjoy what you now have. When you first put your trust in Me, I forgave your past sins and wiped your slate clean. Why then would you constantly chastise yourself with remorse? I have forgiven you, now forgive yourself, completely. Remember, those who have been forgiven much, love much.

With these errors in mind, fix your eyes on the way forward. Fix your eyes on the path set before you. Keep your hands firmly on your "plough", that is your own calling, given to you by Me. As you do so, I walk alongside you to guide and strengthen you.

Today do not look back but press on to your high calling. I will show you the way to go.

Scripture:

If anyone is in Christ, he is a new creation, old things have passed away; behold all things have become new. 2 Corinthians 5:17.

"No one, having put his hand to the plough, and looking back, is fit for the Kingdom of God. Luke 9:62.

Prayer

Thank You Lord, that I am a new creation, the old has gone. Help me to fix my eyes on You and look to the goal of my heavenly calling. You have given me freedom from the power of sin and death, may I walk in it with joy and thanksgiving. Amen.

Questions:

1. How do you regard your old life?

2. Do you ever wish to go back to your former ways?

3. Do you truly appreciate that you have been rescued from the wrath of God?

97: Are You Weary and Heavy-Laden?

Come to Me when you are weary and heavy-laden. So often the cares of the world press upon you, not just your own cares but those of others also. As you see My face, you will find that rest for your soul that you need. Bring all of your worries and speak them out to Me, hand them over so that I take the responsibility. Listen for words of guidance that I may give you for any action that you need to take and resolve to do it. Take My yoke upon your shoulders, it is light and easy to bear. Together I am there beside you and will never forsake you. You are never alone with your cares.

As you come to Me with your prayers and requests, come with a thankful heart, and with praise for what I can do. Trust Me in all things and My peace, which passes human and understanding, will guard your heart and mind.

My peace will guard you from the taunts of the enemy. He always lies and tries to bring you into despair and unbelief. Resist him with My words and he will flee.

You were designed for an abundant life. It is for your freedom that I came to set you free, from the clutches of the enemy and a life of burdens. The cross has accomplished miraculous works for mankind. All your sin was laid on Me and all your burdens can be laid at the foot of the cross.

Whom the Son sets free, is free indeed.

Scripture:

Come to Me all you who are weary and heavy-laden and I will give you rest. Take my yoke upon you ... and you will find rest for your souls. For my yoke is easy and my burden is light. Matthew 11:28-30.

Let us not grow weary while doing good, for in due season we shall reap if we do not lose heart. Galatians 6:9.

Prayer

Forgive me Lord, when I take false responsibility upon myself. Today I choose to hand over my cares and worries to You. I put them at the foot of the cross and ask You to take them. I put my trust in You. Amen.

Questions:

1. What burdens are you carrying today?

2. Will you lay them down for Jesus to pick up and carry?

3. What is the easy yoke that you can put on instead of a heavy one?

98: A "Far Country"

I have said, "I will never leave you", but it is possible for you to leave Me. I have given you a free will because I want your love and devotion to be freely given. Should you turn from Me and walk away, I will never cease to love you. But you may wander in your heart to a "far country". There may be many reasons for you to do so. Perhaps the allure and temptations of the world and the flesh lead you astray. Maybe you feel anger towards Me, thinking that I have let you down and not answered your prayers. Other believers may cause you grief and pain and you blame them.

Whatever the cause, the "far country" will never satisfy your inner needs. I have made you for fellowship with Me, a closeness, parent to child and nothing else will do.

I stand as a loving father looking for your return. Therefore, recognise that the husks of the pigpen must be left behind.

Return to Me, My arms are open to embrace you. I remove the dirty rags of sin and cover you with My robe of righteousness, purchased for you at the cross. I will also give you a ring for your finger. That signet ring represents the seal of My Holy Spirit. He will fill you and empower you, strengthen you to live as I designed you.

Finally, on your feet I give you the shoes of the gospel of peace which enable you to walk in My ways and stay on the true path of everlasting life. Turn to Me child, with your whole heart. I love you and long for closeness with you.

Scripture:

Not many days after, the youngest son gathered all together, journeyed to a far country and wasted his possessions with prodigal living. Luke 15:13

"Return to Me," says the lord of hosts, "and I will return to you." Zechariah 1:3.

Prayer

Lord, help me to stay close to You and to walk in Your ways. Keep me from wandering away from You. I know that in You there is security and purpose. May I never be tempted by a "far country". Amen.

Questions:

1. What is the thing most likely to turn you away from God?

2. Do you blame God when things go wrong?

3. What is your experience of a "far country"?

99: The Hem of His Garment

When the woman with the issue of blood touched the hem of My garment, power went out from Me to her. Today, I say to you, "come to Me, touch the hem of My garment and receive My power".

My power in you enables you to live life well, to live in the way I designed you. As you reach out to Me, you recognise that of yourself you cannot achieve things of eternal worth. My power and My Holy Spirit supply your need. As you put your faith and trust in Me you receive wisdom and guidance for the way you should take. Ask Me for this wisdom both in small things and in big. Things that seem trivial may lead to much greater things, both for good or ill. Therefore, seek My will for you. I ask you to come to Me daily to receive My touch. I desire an intimate fellowship with you not a spasmodic relationship depending on how you feel on any one day. Put your feelings aside and do what is best. Put yourself into My hands, My care and keeping. Learn from Me, listen to Me, receive My great love for you. Speak to Me, bring your requests with thanksgiving. Pray for those in need and place your anxieties onto Me. As you sit at My feet you choose the better part, that is allowing the pressures of the world to take second place. Make Me central to all that you think and do, reaching out to Me and "touching my garment" throughout the day. As you recognise My constant presence, you can walk with reassurance and confidence knowing that I am but a whisper away.

Scripture

Now a woman, having a flow of blood for 12 years………touched the border of his garment and immediately the flow of blood stopped……… Jesus said "I perceive power going out from me". Luke 8:43-46.

Prayer

Lord, help me to keep You at the centre of my life. May everything revolve around You and Your will for me. Show me how to do this because I realise that You know best. Today, may I "touch the hem of Your garment". Amen.

Questions:

1. What do you understand by touching the hem of Jesus' garment?

2. How much will you include Jesus into your life today?

3. Where do you particularly need his strength today?

100: The Perfect Sacrifice

Today, consider the magnitude of My leaving the glory of Heaven to come down to the earth as a man. I willingly chose to leave the status of the Godhead to take the form of a lowly servant. I came not to a palace but to a humble family. I did not seek reputation and standing but only to do the will of My Father.

I came willingly to be the final perfect sacrifice for the sins of mankind. There was no other way, the shedding of blood was necessary. For the joy set before Me, I endured the rejection and humiliation, the pain and the torture. I did it for love.

I ask you now to have that same humility, not thinking too highly of yourselves but esteeming others. Have a servant heart, not wanting always to be served but ready to put yourself out for those in need.

Do not work for the praise of men but for My ultimate "well done". Do your good works without wishing to be seen and rewarded.

Dig out the treasures of your salvation. There is so much more than a home in Heaven. You are being saved in the present. Rescued from the clutches of the enemy. Seek to live your life as a demonstration of what you have been given. Be light in a dark world. Be salt in a tasteless generation. Live a life of faith and trust. A life of thanksgiving and peace and joy in the Holy Spirit. By doing so, you become part of that joy set before Me, making My sacrifices totally worthwhile.

Scripture:

Jesus Christ humbled Himself and became obedient to death, even the death of the cross. Philippians 2:8.

Looking unto Jesus, the author and finisher of our faith, who for the joy that was set before Him endured the cross. Hebrews 12:2.

Prayer

Gracious Lord, thank You for Your great love for us which brought You to the earth as a sacrifice for our sin. How amazing is Your grace and mercy. I am eternally grateful.

Questions:

1. Do you have a servant heart, or do you prefer to be served?

2. Can you begin to comprehend the enormity of Christ's sacrifice?

3. How will you demonstrate your gratitude today?

101: The God of "How Much More"

I am the God of "How much more". Consider My ways and thoughts. How much more mighty are they than your thoughts and ways. I am the Creator seeing all and knowing all, how much more will I give back to you, good measure, pressed down, shaken together and running over.

I love a cheerful giver and will gladly supply much more in return. I am the God of abundance, the cattle on every hill, the wealth in every mine. I love to give in large measure.

You come to Me because I have the words of eternal life and I give you so much more. I give you abundant life. A life of joy and peace in the Holy Spirit. A life of security where you have self-worth and significance, a child of the living God.

When you give Me your five loaves and two fish, whatever this represents to you, how much more will I multiply your offering. I can use a little to become much. A little love and kindness can mean more than you imagine to those who are suffering. Be generous with your time and your love. How much more will I use your little.

Also, if you, being evil, know how to give good gifts to your children, how much more will I give the Holy Spirit to those who ask Me. You come to Me empty-handed, but I will fill you and supply your need from My glorious riches. You love Me, but how much more I love you, My precious child.

Scripture:

Now, to Him who is able to do exceedingly abundantly above all that we ask or think…….. to Him be glory. Ephesians 3:20-21.

"If you then, being evil, know how to give good gifts to your children, how much more will your Heavenly Father give the Holy Spirit to those who ask Him!" Luke 11:13.

Prayer

Lord, enlarge my thinking of who You are and what You are able to do. So often I make You too small, too much like me and too limited. I praise You today because You are the one true living God, Creator and Saviour. The God of "How much more". Amen.

Questions:

1. In what areas of your life do you limit God?

2. Where do you need His, "how much more"?

3. Do you believe that God will be, "so much more" to you personally?

102: Our Perfect Parent

I ask you to come to Me with childlike faith and trust. I am a perfect parent, unlike earthly parents who are subject to their feelings and can make bad judgements. I, however, know the way that you should take, what is best for you, what you can achieve.

It is impossible for you to understand everything about Me or My creation. The clay is subject to the Potter. I am the Potter, you are the clay. Therefore, be willing to let Me shape and mould you without demanding to know the reason for everything.

Do you want a God who is equal to you? A God that you can put in a box and contain? It is impossible. My understanding is unsearchable. People make great discoveries about the working of the world and see themselves as God, forgetting that I gave them intelligence and formed the earth with the word of My mouth. I laugh from heaven as a doting parent laughing at the child who takes his first steps.

In My love for you, I chasten you when you go astray. I seek to keep you on your true path and gently guide you with My Shepherd's rod and staff.

My word given to you is of great worth. It contains all you need for life and godliness. You will not understand all that it contains. For example, future things are withheld so that you remain ready and alert for My return. Hold fast to the truth that I have revealed to you, so that you stand firm and walk in My ways. You are My precious child, and I will always love you.

Scripture:

The creator of the ends of the earth, neither faints nor is weary. His understanding is unsearchable. Isaiah 40:28.

A man's heart plans his way, but the Lord directs his steps. Proverbs 16:9.

Prayer

Lord, I thank You that You are so much higher, mightier and more amazing than I can ever understand. You are God and I am made by You. Please show me Your path and direct my way today. Amen.

Questions:

1. Do you make plans then ask God to bless them?

2. How often do you seek God's will for your day?

3. Do you make God in your image and thus limit him?

103: Access to the King

Many years ago, when Esther the Queen sought an audience with the king, she risked her very life. She had to wait and see if he would extend his Sceptre towards her in acceptance, or not, meaning death. I am the King above all kings, but unlike earthly monarchs, I bid you come to Me boldly, night and day. I am always available to speak with you and to listen to you.

When I died on the cross, at My final breath, the curtain of the temple was torn from top to bottom, from Heaven to earth. Prior to My sacrifice, the high priest could only enter once a year and that bearing blood which he offered as an atonement for his own sins and those of the people. Now that former covenant has been replaced by the new. I call you to come boldly to My throne of Grace, to have a close and intimate fellowship with Me. It grieves My heart when My children take this privilege lightly or for granted. Some come to Me only when they have a need. Others may meet up weekly to sing and pray and ignore Me for the other 6 days. This was not My plan for you. I want you to know Me more as I know you, to spend time with Me daily, sitting in My presence listening for My still small voice and talking to Me, heart to heart.

When Ester came to the King, it resulted in a nation being saved. When you come to Me and love and worship it results in you carrying My presence with you into a needy world and perhaps saving a soul. Make My joy complete and become aware of My walk with you throughout the day. I am for you not against you. Enjoy your walk with Me.

Scripture:

Eshter said, "I will go to the King, which is against the law and if I perish, I perish! Esther 4:16.

Jesus cried out again with a loud voice and yielded up His Spirit. Then behold, the veil of the temple was torn in two from top to bottom. Matthew 27:50-51.

Prayer

Lord, it is an amazing privilege to be able to come into Your presence at any time. May I never take this for granted or abuse it. Today I draw near to You in the sure and certain knowledge that You will draw near to me Thank You so much. Amen.

Questions

1. Do you make an audience with your King a priority?

2. How important is this to you really?

3. What will you talk to your King about today?

104: But God…

Is your glass half empty or half full? Do you see the negative rather than the positive? Do you worry about the worst things that may happen? Have you a fear of loss, loss of health, loss of finance and so on and on. If and when such fears and negative thoughts come to you, have the words, "BUT GOD" at the ready. Never count Me out, count Me in, into every situation and every difficulty that arises. Consider My Word about when you were dead in your old life. You were once in sin, "BUT GOD", who is rich in mercy made you alive! You were given a new, abundant life of peace and joy.

You could not save yourself, BUT GOD died in your place as the necessary sacrifice. Meditate on the greatness and power of the cross and My unconditional love for you. It will put negative thoughts into perspective and transform your mind. My word is given to encourage and strengthen you. Hold fast to My promises.

I am God your provider. I will give you what you need when the time comes. Wait patiently on Me and I will renew your strength. I will lead and guide you in the way you should go. When trials and tribulations arise, know that I am with you even in the darkest valley and I will uphold you with My righteous right hand. Do not allow the lies of Satan to bring you down, causing you to doubt Me. Hold onto what you learn in the light and say no to dark, imagining. Resist the devil and he will flee.

Press on child, your glass is more than half full, it is running over with the water of my life. Therefore, rejoice in all you have and live an abundant life.

Scripture:

But God, who is rich in mercy because of his great love.... made us alive together with Christ. Ephesians 2:4-5.

I have come that you may have life, and have it more abundantly. John 10:10.

Prayer

Forgive me Lord, when I entertain negative thoughts. You have given me fullness of life in Christ, and I choose today to focus on Your mercy and grace towards me. Strengthen me and uphold me and teach me to resist the lies of the enemy. Amen.

Questions
1. Is your glass half full or half empty?

2. Do you have a tendency to have negative thoughts and worry about the future?

3. How can you replace negative thinking with what is helpful?

105: The "God-Shaped" Blank

There is in each person a "God shaped" blank that only I can fill. Without Me, there is an emptiness inside. People attempt to fill this with wrong gods of many kinds. The world tempts with various different things but all of them fall short. None will satisfy the deep longing of the heart. The enemy whispers lies, "If only you could have this"; "If only could do that"; or, "Follow another god and then you will know happiness and success". Such things only last for a short while and their promise is never fulfilled.

Because I designed and created you, I know you inside out. I know how you should function and what you need to live well. It is only as you come to Me and put your hand into Mine, that you find the very thing that you have been searching for, peace with Me and therefore peace in your heart.

Such peace cannot be found in material things or even family and friends. It is a blank shape that only I can fill.
When you wander away from Me, you experience a loss, an unease that you cannot put your finger on. It is necessary to stay close to Me. Stay in harmony and communion with Me to know that peace which passes all understanding.

I delight in you, My child, and I too, feel that loss when you are not in touch with Me. Make My joy complete, love Me and love one another and know the deep joy that only I can give.

Scripture:

The heart is restless until it finds its rest in Thee. Saint-Augustine.

Little children keep yourselves from idols. 1 John 5:21.

Prayer

Lord, thank You, that when I stay close to You I know Your peace and joy. Please help me to follow only You as my blueprint for life. May I find in You all that I need. Amen.

Questions:

1. What are the things, or people that you might look to for satisfaction?

2. Do you recognise the peace that only God can give?

3. Today, will you turn from any "idols" and seek to follow God's way for you?

106: You are the Temple for the Holy Spirit

When I went into the Temple court and saw the money changers and those who were buying and selling, My anger was aroused. They were making My Father's house into a den of thieves. In My anger, I drove them out and overturned the tables that they were using. You have been bought with a costly price and have become a temple for My Holy Spirit. Therefore, do not allow yourselves to be used by the enemy for setting up tables, his tables, in your life. These may consist of many and varied things, whatever would hinder you, the enemy knows. Is there unforgiveness in your heart? It will lead to a bitter root in your soul, and you must turn over this table. Forgive as you have been forgiven and allow Me to take retribution when necessary.

Is there any doubt and fear in your heart or even unbelief? This is a table that the enemy loves to sit at, to trade in his lies and deception. Turn it over and trust in Me. Give Me your fears and worries, cast them on to Me and walk in freedom. Do not exchange truth for a lie, do not buy into them. Take stock today of your temple, your heart and soul. Turn over anything that is not of Me, anything that would hinder your walk with Me and prevent you from becoming the person I designed you to be.

You are worth so much to Me and I want the very best for you. So, turn and repent of anything that grieves My Holy Spirit that you may be full of love and joy.

Scripture

Jesus went into the Temple of God and drove out all those who bought and sold in the Temple and overturned the tables of the money changers. Matthew 21:12.

...with regard to your former way of life, put off your old self... and put on the new self, created to be like God. Ephesians 4:22&24

Prayer

Lord God, show me where the enemy has set up any "table" within me, anything that would hinder my walk with You. Create in me a clean heart and lead me on the best path, the path of Your leading. Amen.

Questions:

1. Will you now ask the Lord to show you where the enemy has a foothold in you?

2. Can you repent of anything that is needful and ask God to fill you?

3. How can you prevent the enemy from setting up "tables" in your life?

107: Sitting at Jesus's Feet

I don't want you to come into My presence as a duty but a pleasure. Come, knowing the great love that I have for you. I want the very best for your life and that can only come through Me. You were made for communion with Me, so being still, knowing that I am God, fulfils this purpose. You receive a sense of belonging, a rightful place at My side and the security that I provide.

Sitting at My feet as Mary did, you learn My ways and My thoughts toward you. I will teach you and guide you in the way you should go. I will also gently steer you onto the right path if you are in danger of going astray. As a Good Shepherd, I watch over you and keep you safe. The enemy goes around like a roaring lion searching out the weak and the isolated. Apart from Me, you are vulnerable to his attacks. With Me, you learn to discern his lies and resist his temptations.

As you rest in My presence, you experience the peace that I give, peace that passes all understanding but once known, you will never wish to lose.

Being at the centre of My will is the very best and safest place to be. My will is perfect, so spending time quietly listening for My voice you learn to sense what that will is. In that way I also equip you to fulfil My purposes for you. I will never ask you to do something without the means to do it. With these thoughts in mind, enjoy precious time with Me so that together we become one in heart and spirit.

Scripture:

"The chief end of man is to worship God and enjoy Him forever". The Westminster catechism.

Your ears shall hear a word behind you, saying, "this is the way, walk in it". Isaiah 30:21.

Prayer

Lord, I know that the best and safest place to be is at the centre of Your will. Show me Your path today and fill me with Your strength. May my time with You be my priority. Amen.

Questions:

1. Do you have a regular time and place to spend in God's presence?

2. How much of a priority is this for you?

3. Can you sense in your spirit anything that God might be saying to you today?

108: Treasure in Heaven

Your life does not consist in the abundance of your possessions. You brought nothing into the world, and you will certainly take nothing out with you. It is a true saying that, "there are no pockets in shrouds". So do not lay up for yourselves treasure on earth which is transitory. It is futile to trust earthly wealth for your security when things can change in a day and all the wealth in the world cannot buy what you really need.

Instead of looking to hoard your possessions, lay up yourself treasure in Heaven. Hold what you have loosely. Be willing to give and to share. The things of earth will all pass away but the things of Heaven will endure for eternity. How much better for you to consider eternity, for where your treasure is, there will your heart be.

This world is not your home. Your true home is prepared for you in My Father's house. There is room for you there to be all that you were designed to be, with no more pain or suffering.

As you meditate on this, the things of earth and the here-and-now will be put into perspective. All the possessions that man seeks after, seem trivial in comparison to your ultimate inheritance. That inheritance will never fade, it is priceless and is reserved in heaven for you. The currency of Heaven is not in silver and gold but in love, joy and peace in the Holy Spirit. Therefore, how much better for you to look to your Heavenly treasure than to scurry around laying up wealth on earth which will one day be of no value whatsoever.

Scripture:

Take heed and beware of covetousness, for one's life does not consist in the abundance of the things he possesses. Luke 12:15.

Do not lay up for yourselves treasure on earth……… but lay up for yourselves treasure in Heaven. Matthew 6:19-20.

Prayer

Lord, help me to find my security in You and not in my possessions or finance. Give me a generous heart that is willing to share what I have. May my treasure be in Heaven. Amen.

Questions:

1. Where does your security lie?

2. Are you able to share what you have?

3. What legacy would you like to leave on earth when you die?

109: Dealing with Shame

When I died on the cross, I took upon Myself not only your sin but your shame. I was able to do this as the spotless Lamb of God.

As you come to Me in repentance for your sins, give Me also the shame that you carry. All have sinned, from the greatest to the lowest. All fall short of my glory. Thus, there is a need to recognise your weakness and My power.

Shame is something that may linger in your heart and mind even after you have received forgiveness. This shame can be used against you by the enemy to bring you down, causing you to lack self-worth. It can feel like a blanket of condemnation which only I can remove. Allow Me to take that shame, that blanket and replace it with My robe of righteousness.

Do not dwell on the past, all that you now regret. The old has gone, the new has come. You are a new creation born again by My Holy Spirit. Nothing needs to be wasted in My economy. Use the things of the past to help others. When someone is suffering in whatever kind of trial, only those who have suffered with the same can truly understand and sympathise. Therefore, use your past to be a catalyst for change in others. Thwart the plans of the enemy by bringing light where there is darkness.

As far as the East is from the West is how far I have taken your sins from you. Therefore, hold up your head. My hand is under your chin. Walk in the strength that I give you and leave your shame at the cross.

Scripture:

Looking unto Jesus, the author and finisher of our faith, who… endured the cross, despising the shame, and has sat down at the right hand of the throne of God. Hebrews 12:2.

Whoever believes in him will never be put to shame. Romans 10:11.

Prayer

Thank You Lord, that when You died for us, You took not only our sin but also our shame. Thank You Lord, that I can now live in newness of life, set free from all past shame.

Questions:

1. Do you still carry shame from your past?

2. Do you truly believe that Jesus died for your shame as well as your sin?

3. What scripture will you use to turn away the taunts of Satan regarding shame?

110: This is the Way

Are you someone who always wants your own way, thinking you know best for yourself and others? However, have you ever set off to go somewhere convinced that you are going in the right direction only to find that you are on the wrong road, heading for a different destination?

This can also be a metaphor for the choices you make in life. You may make a decision, but soon come to realise this was a mistake. How much better to follow a map or a guide for any journey you have to make. How much better also for you to have a map and a guide for other choices. Since I created you, I know what is best for you and what would harm you. I am the Good Shepherd who can lead and guide you in paths of righteousness.

My word is the map for your life. It is also a light to your path. In it are the directions and signposts to help you. As you follow My truths you will hear that voice behind you saying, "this is the way, walk in it". The world, the flesh and the devil all call out to you, "follow me, choose my ways, take care of number one and don't worry about your neighbour".

I have given you free will and allow you to choose your own path, but My greatest desire is for you to choose to follow Me, to love Me, to have a close relationship with Me, not because you must but because you may. So today I say to you, who will you choose? As you choose to follow Me, I will be with you and uphold you because I love you.

Scripture:

Your word is a lamp to my feet and a light to my path. Psalm 119:105.

Your ears shall hear a word behind you, saying, "this is the way, walk in it". Isaiah 30:21.

Prayer

Thank You so much for Your precious word, Lord. May I cherish it and follow its directions. You know the way that I should take. Help me to listen for that still small voice that guides and keeps me. Amen.

Questions:

1. How important is God's word to you?

2. How often do you read it?

3. Do you allow it to guide your way of life and your attitudes?

111: Joy Comes in the Morning

Weeping may endure for a night, but joy comes in the morning. In your earthly life you will suffer many things, sadness, sorrow, pain, bereavement, and loss. Such is the lot of mankind. No one is exempt from these things. When you pass through these storms or the valley of the shadow of death, draw ever nearer to Me. Then is not the time to turn from Me, blame Me and say I do not care. Sadly, you live in a fallen world where bad things happen.

I suffered during My time on earth, was scorned and rejected, suffered the agony of the cross. I understand. You are not alone. Stay close to Me, be angry but do not sin. Do not let the sun go down on your wrath. Though you have that "night" of weeping, remember that joy will come in due time if you hold fast to Me.

I endured suffering for the joy set before Me. You too, can look to the time when you will be free from tears, pain and loss, in your home in heaven for eternity. When you go through tribulation, keep your heart pure. Do not let bitterness take root, it will spring up, cause trouble and hinder others. Blame and unforgiveness can be like poison to your soul, harming only yourself. Forgive, when necessary, just as you have been forgiven. Asking the question, "why?" is a fruitless exercise, you may never receive an answer.

Consider My servant Job, in all his trials, he did not sin or blame Me for anything. Follow his example that the trial of your faith might be found to be to His praise and glory and honour at My appearing.

Scripture:

Weeping may endure for a night, but joy comes in the morning. Psalm 30:5.

He was despised and rejected by men, a Man of Sorrows and acquainted with grief. Isaiah 53:3.

Prayer

Lord God, thank You that You are always with me, in joy and in sorrow. You know what it is like to suffer, You endured all that sinful man would do. Please help me to stay close at all times, in good times and in bad. Amen.

Questions:

1. What is your reaction when you suffer?

2. Are you someone who often says, "Why me"?

3. When you are "squeezed" what comes out?

112: Our Purpose and Work

I made you on purpose and for purpose. I created you in love and prepared work for you to do. Everyone needs purpose and work to do. There is a true saying, "the devil finds work for idle hands".

Do not confuse the work that I give you to do with trying to earn your salvation. You could never achieve that of yourself, it is My gift to you, purchased not with silver or gold, but with My own blood shed on the cross. No, the work that I delegate to you is for furthering My Kingdom. When I give you work, I will equip you to do it. When you use your gifting, you will not have to struggle and strive. Rather you will find satisfaction and fulfilment in what you do.

Some things that I give you to do may seem trivial in the eyes of the world. Remember this however, that you are part of My body, and every cell has its purpose. Some people are equipped to be teachers or evangelists, but others are called to work behind the scenes, unnoticed by others but seen by Me. I love a servant's heart. I Myself came not to be served but to serve. Therefore, be assured that whatever you do for the least of My brethren you do for Me.

In all that you do, ensure that you abide in Me, as a branch of the Vine. Dwelling with Me and in Me will enable you to bear good fruit, fruit that lasts.

So today, ask of Me, "what would you have me do?", "whom can I bless?" I will give you your work and enable you to do it with joy.

Scripture:

For we are His workmanship, created in Christ Jesus for good works, which God prepared beforehand that we should walk in them. Ephesians 2:10.

Show me your faith without your works, and I will show you my faith by my works. James 2:18.

Prayer

Lord, thank You that You have made me for good works. I know that they do not save me but are things that You have planned for me to fulfil. Thank You that whatever You ask of me You will equip me to do. Amen.

Questions:

1. What has God given you to do at this time?

2. Are you prepared to be used by God for his purposes?

3. Will you seek Him today for your mission big or small?

113: Saved by Grace Alone

I came to the earth to be the good news, the Gospel of Salvation. I came on purpose to die for the sins of the world, to take the punishment due to you, upon Myself. I died and rose again, death was defeated!

As you come to Me in faith and receive Me to yourself, you are born again of My Spirit. Faith in My sacrifice for you is the way and the truth and life itself. Do not be seduced by other false gospels. These will lead you from the true path of life. For example, you cannot earn your salvation through good works. All have sinned and fall short of My glory. Neither can you be saved from the wrath to come by any religious ritual. The good news is that you are saved by My Grace, through faith and not of yourself. You cannot boast about your good works as if they are sufficient. I am the only way, the only one, who can give you life eternal.

As you put your faith in My death and resurrection, your old life will end and a new life begins. My Holy Spirit is given to empower you to live the life that I planned for you from the foundation of the world, a life that will give you purpose and joy.

There is in man the desire to be self-sufficient, to do things his own way. But I say to you, find your sufficiency in Me. I am enough. do things My way and you will find it is the very best way. Accept the fact that a sacrifice for sin was necessary, but that you need to respond in faith, herein is the true Gospel. It will give you life and peace and everlasting joy, a relationship with Me forever.

Scripture:

If anyone preaches any other gospel to you than what you have received, let him be accursed. Galatians 1:9.

For it is by grace you have been saved through faith, and this not from yourselves, it is the gift of God, not of works, so that no one can boast. Ephesians 2:8-9.

Prayer

Lord, I accept that I cannot earn my salvation. Thank You that it is Your gift, precious and costly to You, but free to me. May I walk in the good of this today. knowing that You are for me and that You love me perfectly. Amen.

Questions

1.Do you still ever seek to earn your salvation?

2. Does your old, former life ever call you to go back?

3.Will you spend time today thanking God for this amazing gift?

114: Christ at the Centre

Picture your life as a house with various rooms, built up of body, soul and spirit. Much of your house will be concerned with your daily activities, duties to perform and work to be done. Include Me in these mundane things, speak to Me as you go about your daily life. I want to be part of your work, rest, and leisure.

Pause for a moment and consider whether there is a basement room in your life which holds bad memories or things of which you are ashamed. You keep this door firmly locked. I say to you today, open it to Me, give Me entrance that My light can shine in and clean it up and bring healing. I can deal with your past hurts, rejection, and abuse, pouring in the balm of My Holy Spirit. Where you are ashamed, seek My forgiveness and be restored. Walk in freedom from your past, keep nothing locked away where it will fester.

Is there another room which is labelled, "hopes and dreams"? Bring these desires to Me. I can give you those wishes that are in your heart according to My will for you. I long for you to find fulfilment and purpose. My plans for you are good and perfect and acceptable. Ask Me, seek Me and find Me in your dreams. Have you a room where your unanswered prayers are kept? When you pray and seek My will and keep on praying. I hear your prayers, but some things are not right for you and others take time, my timing is always the best. Do not give up.

Finally, do not have a room which is just for worship of Me. I want to have access to your whole house and not to be confined. Make Me the centre of all you do and your house will stand firm and secure through calm and storm.

Scripture:

Whether you eat or drink, or whatever you do, do all for the glory of God. 1 Corinthians 10:31.

For I know the thoughts that I think towards you says the Lord, thoughts of peace and not of evil, to give you a future and a hope. Jeremiah 29:11.

Prayer

Thank You Lord, that You are for me and want the best for me. Please come into every part of my life, every "room". May there be nothing that I try to keep from You. Fill every part with Your Holy Spirit that I may walk in Your ways. Amen.

Questions:

1. Do you keep God just for Sundays?

2. Have you deep hurts and memories that need healing?

3. Will you allow God into your whole life for His plans and purposes?

115: Bear With One Another

Bear with one another in love. Make allowances for each other. I made you as individuals, not mass-produced. Each person has his or her own character, thoughts, strengths, and weaknesses. Some people are outgoing while others are introverts. No one is perfect, no one is free from sin, no one attains My standard. Therefore, keep this in mind when you become irritated with a fellow believer. Bear with him or her and do not let words or actions cause strife. Do not pass on this irritation or offence to others as gossip or backbiting. You do not know and cannot know each person's background, trials, and worries, just as they do not know yours. Therefore, see your irritability as your own problem to be dealt with and as a stepping-stone towards maturity.

Bear with one another, and also forgive one another when you have been hurt, offended or maligned. Come to Me with your grievance first and foremost, before any root of bitterness creeps in. Allow Me to be the judge of others. I am the Lord and if there is just cause, I will repay for the harm.

Forgive as I have forgiven you and let no poison of unforgiveness come between us. Choose to forgive, rather than waiting to feel like it. That will probably never come. My aim is for unity and harmony amongst My children. Therefore, keep the bond of peace in humility and love, being thankful for all your blessings.

As you let My word dwell in you richly, it will give you wisdom and understanding. Follow My example and just as I bear with you, bear with each other and love wholeheartedly.

Scripture:

Put on tender mercies,... bearing with one another, and forgiving one another. Colossians 3:12-13.

Make love your aim. 1 Corinthians 14:1.

Prayer

Lord, please forgive me when I think ill of others, become irritated or judge. Give me a heart of love like Yours. May I seek peace and pursue it and attempt to bring unity where there is discord. Amen.

Questions:

1. Are you quick to judge?

2. Do you readily make allowances for yourself but not for others?

3. How do you react to irritations and annoyances?

116: The Lord's Table

There is room at My table for all who have come to Me in faith. I do not look at external things such as colour of skin, gender, age, or intellect. I look at the heart, is it a heart after Me?

While you wait for that great feast in the Heavenly Kingdom, remember Me on earth. Remember that last supper that I had with My disciples and do likewise.

Break bread together knowing that I, the Bread of Life, gave My body to be broken for you on the cross. As bread is taken into your body, allow Me also to become part of you. The cup speaks of My blood shed for you. Without the shedding of blood there can be no forgiveness for sin. My sacrifice was the final perfect offering. The old order of animal sacrifices was ended, surpassed by the new covenant. The law was unable to save but now the new promise welcomes all who call upon My Name in faith to be saved.

Do these things in remembrance of Me until My return to earth. I have promised to come back and will never break a promise.

As you wait, what manner of people should you be? Be ready with your lamps filled with My Holy Spirit. He is given to guide, comfort and be your helper in this life.

Live a life of love for all. Be steadfast and unmovable and abound in the work that I give you to do, knowing that I am with you and for you.

Scripture:

The Lord Jesus took bread and when He had given thanks, He broke it and said, "take, eat this is My body which is broken for you. Do this in remembrance of Me". 1 Corinthians 11:24.

Jesus said, "I AM the bread of life". John 6:35.

Prayer

Thank You Lord, that You call us to Your table, that we may eat the bread of Life. Thank You that Your body was broken so that we could be made whole. Amen.

Questions:

1. Can you truly say that you have a heart that is after God?

2. Have you called upon the name of the Lord to be saved and trust daily in Him?

3. Is your lamp filled? That is, with the Holy Spirit?

117: Grace, Mercy and Peace

Grace, mercy and peace to you. Herein is the very essence of My love for you. I extended My grace to you even while you were in sin. I reached out to you with My favour when you did not deserve it. Since you could never earn your salvation, it had to come through My grace. Through My grace towards you, I died for you, instead of you, taking your sin upon Myself.

My grace does not end with salvation, but everyday I pour out My grace in ways that you often fail to recognise. Every breath and every blessing is by My grace, My unmerited favour. Likewise, My mercy is extended to you daily. Through My mercy you are kept from the punishment for sin that you deserved and My mercy continues, setting you free and allowing you to enjoy the benefits of an abundant life.

As you begin to understand the great love that I have for you, not only in dying for you, but in continuing to be seen in My grace and mercy, you are able to experience My peace.

My peace is deep and unfathomable. It passes understanding. It allows you to live your life free from fear, knowing that your times are in My hands. Peace in the world begins with peace in the heart. It is a precious fruit that comes from abiding in Me, drawing strength and purpose as you live close to Me.

Do not permit the world and its ways to rob you of the peace that I died to give you. Look daily for the signs of My grace and mercy towards you, being thankful and so let My peace guard your heart and mind.

Scripture:

Let us come to the throne of Grace, that we may obtain mercy and find grace to help in time of need. Hebrews 4:16.

And the peace of God, which surpasses all understanding, will guard your hearts and mind through Christ Jesus. Philippians 4:7.

Prayer

Lord, thank You for Your grace, Your mercy and Your peace. Intangible things that make a world of difference to our lives. Your blessings are new every morning and I rejoice in the knowledge that You love me. Amen.

Questions:

1. In what ways has God shown His grace to you?

2. Do you recognise the fact that God's mercy has saved you?

3. How do you maintain the peace of God daily?

118: The Elder Brother

Rejoice with those who rejoice and mourn with those who mourn. Which of these do you find easier to do?

When others receive praise and blessings are you always delighted or is there a part of you that feels envious?

Consider the elder brother of the prodigal son. The latter had wasted his inheritance and behaved shamefully, yet on his return was greeted by his father with great joy. Instead of being pleased at this, the elder brother was filled with resentment and envy. He had been faithful and hard-working but felt he was not honoured or recognised. The father was quick to point out that the elder had everything at his disposal, he could have killed a fatted calf at any time! He had a robe and a ring and sandals already. He lacked nothing.

When others are blessed or have food fortune, do you rejoice deep down? Is there a part of you that says, "what about me?" I say to you, do not have that elder brother spirit. Know that you are deeply loved and that I recognise all your deeds and hard work. I provide you with all you need for life and godliness. Should you feel overlooked, remember that I see all and know all. Your reward may not be great on earth but will be great in Heaven.
I look on the heart, so repent of any ill, feeling, envy and resentment and bless those who are blessed and rejoice with those who rejoice and keep your heart pure.

Scripture:

The older son said, "These many years I have served you, yet you never gave me a young goat!..." The father said, "son you are always with me and all that I have is yours". Luke 15:29-31.

Rejoice with those who rejoice, and weep with those who weep. Romans 12:15.

Prayer

Please Lord, give me a heart like Yours, so that I may rejoice with those who rejoice and love like You. Thank You that everyday, You provide me with all I need, if only I take time to recognise it. Bless the works of my hands this day. Amen.

Questions:

1. Do you feel envy when things go well for others?

2. Will you repent of any such attitudes?

3. Do you look for rewards on earth or in heaven?

119: God Chooses the Weak

When I called Gideon, he said, "my clan is the weakest ,and I am the least in my father's house". Thus, he was the perfect candidate to fulfil My plans.

I choose the weak things of the world and the foolish to confound the so-called wise. Since I will not give My Glory to another, I look for those who are humble of heart, those who refuse to boast in their own achievements. David was a young shepherd boy when I chose him to become a king. He too, was the least in his father's house and scorned by his brothers, but I saw that his heart was "after Me", and he finally became a great leader.

When someone with addiction can finally admit, "I am powerless", that is the time when the higher power can begin to work. I am the highest of all powers, higher than kings, lords and rulers. I am also the most merciful and compassionate. I seek to save the least, the last and the lost. These weakest who are saved are the ones who know Me best. The ones forgiven the most, love the most.

Therefore, if you consider yourself to be unworthy and of little value, welcome into my army, mighty warrior. You are the one who will seek to stay close, keeping your eye out for any commands and submitting to My leadership. Together we can do exploits, to bring life where there is death, light where there is darkness and joy where there is despair.

Always remember My strength is made perfect in your weakness.

Scripture:

Gideon said, "Oh my lord, how can I save Israel? Indeed, my clan is the weakest in Manasseh, and I am the least in my father's house". Judges 6:15.

He said, "My grace is sufficient for you, for My strength is made perfect in weakness". 2 Corinthians 12:9.

Prayer

Lord, I realise that Your Kingdom is very different to the ways of the world. Thank You that You chose the weak, those who know that they really need You. Please make me humble in heart so that You can use me for Your glory. Amen.

1. How do you feel about yourself?

2. Do you recognise your weaknesses?

3. Will you be prepared to be used by God for His purposes today, regardless of your weakness?

120: The Strategy of Satan

From the beginning, the strategy of Satan has been seen. Firstly, the question, "Has God said?" With such words he seeks to sow doubt and unbelief in every heart. No one is immune from such a question and each needs to be ready with an answer.

Since the devil knows our weaknesses, he shapes his questions accordingly. Be alert and when doubts arise, have words of scripture that will speak the truth.

Similarly, the enemy will lie. He is the father of lies and speaks his native language of lies. He sees when you are vulnerable, hurt by someone, tired and heavy laden, isolated or hungry and weak. At such times, his lies may seem like the truth, such as, "God doesn't care about me", or, "I am useless". Consider such thoughts, and remember in the dark, what you learnt in the light.

My word is always your source of reference and truth. Read it daily as your spiritual nourishment. Allow it to go deep into your soul and understanding. It will enable you to discern the truth from lies, enable you to resist the schemes of Satan to disable you. You have purpose in My Kingdom which the enemy always attempts to thwart.

Be strong in the strength I give you. Ask for My Holy Spirit to fill you and guide you. He will lead you into all truth and when the question comes, "has God said?" your answer will be on your lips, "yes, God speaks and He loves me and will never cease to love me".

Scripture:

Now the serpent was more cunning than any beast of the field and he said to the woman, "Has God indeed said ..."? Genesis 3:1.

You will know the truth and the truth will set you free. John 8:32.

Prayer

Lord, help me to guard my heart and mind against the snares, questions and lies of the devil. Make me alert to those times when I am weak and vulnerable, tired, angry, lonely or hungry. May I stay close to You and hear Your truth. Amen.

Questions:

1. When are you personally most vulnerable to the attacks of the enemy?

2. How can you guard your heart and mind?

3. Is there a scripture verse ready in your mind?

121: Have Faith in God

Have faith to believe in Me and that I know best about all things. I hold the world in My hands and sustain everything in it. Therefore, trust Me to know what is best for you also. I am higher than any other, King of kings and Lord of lords. There is no one to compare with Me. I have created all things and by My power I hold all things together.

Do not put your trust in wealth and possessions. Never take your abilities, health, or welfare for granted. Remember the rich man who foolishly said, "I have everything I need. I will take my leisure". He lost all in a day. So with you, your circumstances can change overnight. Therefore, it is vital to stay close to Me, the one who cannot be shaken, who is unchanging and unchangeable. I can hold and sustain you through the storms of life. I am in the boat with you. You will get to the other side.

As a maid watches her mistress for the least sign of her wishes, so keep your eye on Me for My intentions. Keep your ears tuned to My still small voice for your instructions at any time.

My ways and thoughts are far above and beyond the greatest intellect of the world, I gave the intellect! Therefore, look to Me as the one who knows best. Trust Me in all that you think and do. Allow My Holy Spirit within you to teach you, guide you and help you, and you will live at peace with Me, your Creator and Redeemer.

Scripture:

In all your ways acknowledge Him and He will direct your paths. Proverbs 3:6.

He is before all things, and in Him all things hold together. Colossians 1:17.

Prayer

Thank You Lord, that in all the storms of this life I can trust You to be my anchor. I'm so grateful that I have a God who is far above all things yet who knows me intimately. I put my faith and trust in You today. Amen.

Questions:

1. Who do you look to for help when things are difficult?

2. Do you usually think, "I know best, I can cope"?

3. Will you trust God with your whole life today?

122: Prayer

Men ought always to pray and not give up. Prayer is vital to our relationship. It is so much more than just a list of requests to Me.
No, prayer is about spending time in My presence, getting to know the aspects of My character. As you sit with Me, be still and know that I am God. Enter My courts with thanksgiving. Gratitude towards Me for your many blessings will open the doors of Heaven.

As you sit still, "sitting at My feet", ask Me to show you anything that has grieved Me and repent quickly. I am always quick to forgive and restore.
Ask for My Holy Spirit to fill you and worship Me in spirit and in truth. I will be worshipped and have put this desire in mankind. Many worship gods of their own making, but why choose the false when you can have the reality?

I know what you need, but nevertheless, ask Me, as it indicates your dependence on Me for all your needs. Pray for others, asking for discernment in how best to do seek My help for them. Bring your supplications for the world and its great problems, but bring also the small things to Me.

Those that wait upon Me, renew their strength so that they can rise up as on eagles' wings. There you see things from My perspective. You can get to know My heart and My ways. All of these aspects of prayer are about keeping Me at the centre of your life. Therefore, pray without giving up, press on and speak to Me always.

Scripture:

Men ought always to pray and not lose heart. Luke 18:1.

Those who wait on the Lord shall renew their strength, they shall mount up with wings like eagles. They shall run and not be weary they, shall walk and not faint. Isaiah 40:31.

Prayer

Lord, thank You that prayer has many facets. Teach me to pray. Help me to listen as well as speak. May Your Holy Spirit put those things on my heart that need my prayers. Amen.

Questions:

1. What do you consider prayer to be?

2. Do you merely come to God with requests?

3. How much time do you spend waiting upon God?

123: Abide in Christ

Spend your time on the earth wisely and well. If you are unsure of the way you should take, ask Me for wisdom and I will give it to you. Ask in faith, and trust that I desire the best for you. I have come that you may have an abundant life, one that has purpose and gives you a feeling of fulfilment. This comes when you are in the centre of My will.

Do not spend time doing things that are just, "a good idea". People often strive to work for the Kingdom doing things that I have not asked them to do. The good can be the enemy of the best. When you are doing one thing you cannot be doing another and may miss the very thing that I have planned for you. Such activity is as wood, hay and straw, and will be burnt up in the end. Instead, work for the things that endure for eternity, gold, silver and precious stones. These are the works that I have prepared in advance for you to do, works designed for you, works that I will equip you to do.

You know when you are working within your gifting. There is a sense of fulfilment and satisfaction where you do not have to struggle and strive. This is the way that brings peace and joy in your heart.

You can only know My continued guidance by abiding in Me daily. Spend time in My presence and allow My thoughts to become your thoughts. As you abide, so you will bear much fruit, fruit that endures.

Scripture:

Now if anyone builds on this foundation with gold, silver, precious stones, wood, hay, straw, each one's work will become clear. 1 Corinthians 3:12-13.

Abide in Me and I in you. As the branch cannot bear fruit of itself, unless it abides in the vine, neither can you unless you abide in Me. John 15:4.

Prayer

Lord, teach me what it means to abide in You as a branch in the vine. I want to bear fruit, good fruit that endures. May I listen to You for guidance in the things You have planned for me to do. Amen.

Questions:

1. Do you work to gain acceptance by God?

2. How can you, "abide in Christ" daily?

3. What good work do you think God is leading you to do today?

124: A Garment of Praise

I give you a garment of praise instead of a spirit of despair. As you choose to put on a garment, so by an act of your will, "put on" praise. This is a choice which you can make every day.

When trials come, do not be surprised and do not regard them as some kind of punishment. Have I not said, "in the world you will have tribulation"? It is the common lot of man to suffer trials. You live in a fallen world which is groaning for its redemption. High-born and low, rich and poor all have trials in their life. Thus, do not fall into despair. I am with you to comfort you in the dark times. I am the Light of the world so look up to Me. Cast your cares on to Me for I care for you. I weep with you and will bring you through your despair that you may know joy again.

When you find praise difficult, look to the cross. See My pain and suffering and remember that I chose this death because of My great love for you. Praise Me for doing this for you and instead of you. This is a starting point for praise. Then think of the resurrection. I am alive and well with you and in you, praise Me!

Praise Me for sending you the Holy Spirit to guide, and encourage and comfort you. Praise Me for the fact that you have a true home in heaven where you will dwell for eternity, free from pain and tears.

So do not continue in despair. Reach out to Me and know My love. Put on the garment of praise and light will arise.

Scripture

He has sent Me…to bestow on them a crown of beauty instead of ashes… a garment of praise instead of a spirit of despair. Isaiah 61:1,3.

Enter His courts with praise. be thankful to Him and bless His name for the Lord is good. Psalm 100:4-5.

Prayer

Lord, I ask You to create in me a heart of praise. Teach me to praise You at all times, and to use prayers as a weapon against despair and a heavy heart. You are always present with me to comfort so may I lean on You. Amen.

Questions:

1. How do you react to the trials of your life?

2. Do you realise that praise is a powerful weapon against the enemy?

3. Will you put on a garment of praise as a part of your spiritual armour today?

125: The Rock of Ages

When you feel overwhelmed with the things going on around you, take time to be still and know that I am God and that I am in control. The world is full of busyness and rushing, getting and spending. You can be swept along in this fruitless tide. Therefore, come to Me and put things into perspective. What seems so important and pressing today will be much less so in time.

Seek to prioritise what is overwhelming you. What is needful and what is not. Do not allow the enemy to have a toehold into your thinking. He seeks to distract you and turn you away from My plans and purposes for you.

Look to Me, place your feet firmly on the rock of your salvation. I am high above all things; I am all-knowing and all-seeing. I know what lies ahead for you and can keep you safe and secure in My purpose. Put your trust in Me and do not be afraid. I will be with you wherever you go, watching over you, waiting for you to come to Me.

Each person, high born or low, rich and poor, has 24 hours in each day. Be wise with My wisdom and how you spend your time. What is of eternal worth is a plumb line for you to consider in your daily life. Put Me in the centre of all you do and think, and all things can then find their rightful place. Abide in Me, draw up your strength and wisdom from Me, and allow the pressures of life to loosen their grip on you. I am with you and for you, trust in Me alone.

Scripture:

When my heart is overwhelmed, lead me to the Rock that is higher than I. Psalm 61:2.

Come to Him as a living stone, rejected by men but chosen by God and precious. You also, as living stones, are being built up. 1 Peter 2:4-5.

Prayer

Lord, thank You that You are a rock for me, steadfast and sure, never changing or wavering. Today I choose to plant my feet firmly upon You, knowing that I can trust You in all things. Amen.

Questions:

1. How do you cope when you feel overwhelmed?

2. Do you turn to Jesus as a first or last resort?

3. What is causing you anxiety at the moment? Will you put your feet on the Rock?

126: Do Not Grieve the Holy Spirit

I love you with an everlasting love. I made you. I saw you as you were knit together in your mother's womb. I know you entirely, every hair of your head. All your days are written in My book, your coming in, and your going out. Your times are in My hands.

I am your Good Shepherd and seek to lead you into green pastures, that is into My will for you which is the best place for you to be.

Stay close to My side and do not let anything hinder our fellowship. Sin separates us. Since I am a Holy God, I cannot bear to look on sin and it becomes a barrier between us if left. Therefore, allow Me to show you anything in you that would grieve My Holy spirit. Repent quickly and seek forgiveness. I forgive freely, that was My purpose in coming to earth. In this way, channels of communication are kept open. I can gently nudge you into My plans for you and you can speak to Me about all that is in your heart.

Whenever you doubt My love, look to the cross. I suffered and died for you and would die again if I had to, because you are precious in My sight.

Scripture:

Yes, I have loved you with an everlasting love, therefore with loving kindness I have drawn you. Jeremiah 31:3.

Do not grieve the Holy Spirit, by whom you were sealed for the day of redemption. Ephesians 4:30.

Prayer

How can I ever thank You for Your great love, Lord? No words can express the magnitude of Your compassion and mercy. I believe that through this love You chose to die in my place. I am forever grateful, thank You. Amen.

Questions:

1. Do you truly believe that God loves you?

2. When things go wrong, do you think He has withdrawn His love?

3. What act of kindness can you do today to demonstrate God's love in you?

127: The Love of Money

Money is NOT the root of all evil. This is a false saying; the evil is the Love of money. The evil is the desire to have more and more, never being satisfied that you have enough. If you rely on money and possessions for your security, it is a false security. It can be lost in a day. I am your security; I alone can supply your needs according to My riches in glory. Hold your money and possessions with open hands so that you may give to those in need. Give and it will be given you, pressed down and shaken together.

What you receive in return for generosity may not be wealth, but can you put a price on peace and joy and love? No! these things are My currency. They will endure for eternity, the currency of Heaven. Therefore, work for the things that last, that your treasure may be in heaven where there is no moth or rust and no thieves to break in and steal.

I highly esteemed the poor widow who put two small coins into the Treasury. She gave out of her poverty, and I saw her heart. She trusted her Heavenly Father to provide for all her needs. Her generosity has been recorded and remembered through the ages.

I love a cheerful giver, one who seeks to bless others without asking for anything in return. But do not seek to be praised for your giving, in fact, where possible, do it in secret. I, who sees all, will reward you in due time.
Make love your aim and keep your heart right and all else will fall into place.

Scripture:

He saw a poor widow putting in two mites. So He said, "truly I say to you that this poor widow has put in more than all". Luke 21:2-3.

Give and it will be given to you: good measure, pressed down and shaken and running over. For with that same measure that you use it will be measured back to you. Luke 6:38.

Prayer

Lord, please give me a right attitude to money. May I be generous to others and keep my heart right before You. Amen.

Questions:

1. What is your attitude to money?

2. Where is your security?

3. Are you generous, having open hands or rather tight-fisted?

128: The Desires of the Flesh, the Eyes, and the Pride of Life

The things of the world, the desires of the flesh, the desires of the eyes and the pride of life are not from the Father but are at the root of sin.

In the beginning, the woman saw that the forbidden tree was good for food and pleasing to the eyes and desirable for gaining wisdom and she took the fruit and ate it.

Here is the true picture of sin coming to entice each person away from the very source of life, God Himself. The enemy is crafty and knows those things which are seductive to each one. For some it is one thing, for others something different. But the end is the same, to turn you from the true path.

It is therefore important to know your weaknesses, to guard your heart and mind. You once fulfilled the cravings of the flesh and indulged its desires and thoughts. But now, as believers and children of God, put off the old and put on the new. The things of the world are passing away but by doing the will of God you will abide forever.

Furthermore, do not boast about your achievements, the pride of life. All that you are and have, every good gift has come down from the Father of lights. Therefore, do not boast in yourself. Boast in Me and what I have done for you, and I will satisfy the desires of your heart.

Scripture:

For all that is in the world- the lust of the flesh, the lust of the eyes, and the pride of life- is not from the Father but is of the world. 1 John 2:16.

Clothe yourselves with the Lord Jesus Christ and make no provision for the desires of the flesh. Romans 13:14.

Prayer

Lord Jesus, help me to stay focused on You and away from the temptations of the world. Make me alert to the schemes of the enemy to entice me away from You. I know that You alone can satisfy the deepest longings of my heart. Amen.

Questions:

1. What would be your desires of the flesh?

2. Do you have pride in your achievements instead of pride in what God has done for you?

3. How do you, "put off" your old ways and, "put on" Christ?

129: Jesus - The Perfect Sacrifice

In My former Covenant, the age of the Law, I required unblemished sacrifices from My people. Now is the age of grace but I still look for unblemished sacrifices, not of animals, but of praise and worship.

You may ask, "what are 'blemished' sacrifices?" They are those times when you pay Me merely lip-service but your heart is far from Me, the times when you only come to Me, as if it were a duty rather than a blessing, and a privilege.

I ask for your best in all things. Give Me the best time of your day, when you are fresh and clear thinking. The last moments of the day should be a closing prayer, not the only time when you come to My throne.

When I left heaven and came to earth it was to be an unblemished sacrifice, the spotless Lamb of God. I lived as a man but did not sin. Though tempted in every way as you are, I did not succumb to the enemy. I had to be that spotless Lamb at My death. In this way, your sins were covered, and death was defeated.

Give Me the honour I deserve by offering back to Me a pure sacrifice. Present yourselves to Me as such, a living sacrifice, and offer the praise and worship that flows from it.

Scripture:

I beseech you therefore, brethren, by the mercies of God, that you present your bodies as a living sacrifice, holy, acceptable to God, which is your reasonable service. Romans 12:1.

Enter His gates with thanksgiving and into His courts with praise. Psalm 100:4.

Prayer

Lord God, I come to You today and seek to be a blessing to You by giving You myself. Take me as I am Lord, cleanse me from my sin and show me how to give You, "unblemished" worship, that is my best, because You are worthy of all honour and praise. Amen.

Questions:

1. What is your heart attitude in coming to God?

2. Do you give Him your best time of the day?

3. In what ways can you give yourself to the Lord today?

130: Great Oaks from Little Acorns

Do not despise the day of small things. Great oaks grow from little acorns. A small mustard seed can become a tree that the birds can rest in. Even a tiny seed of faith can be powerful for moving the mountains of a trial.

How do you know the effect that a word from your lips may have on a needy person?

When you are born again by My Spirit you are a babe, small in the eyes of the world. Through My word and through your prayers you grow and eventually mature. You are able to be a force for good in My Kingdom. An oak of righteousness for the display of My splendour.

One small part of My word can be a great catalyst for good. One verse may be used to bring a soul to salvation. Another may bring conviction of sin and lead to repentance. Yet another may bring guidance, comfort or reassurance. Small things, but in My hands used to great purpose.

What small thing can you do or say today that may have a great impact on another's life and circumstance? Do not think that anything is too small, any prayer too brief or any kind deed unseen by Me. I can take the small and make it mighty.

Scripture:

For who has despised the day of small things. Zechariah 4:10.

If you have faith the size of a mustard seed, you will say to this mountain, "move from here," and it will move, and nothing will be impossible for you. Matthew 17:20-21.

Prayer

Lord, help me to look for small things that I can do which will impact someone for good. I know that You turned small fish and loaves into so much more. Please fill me today that I may be in tune with Your Holy Spirit. Amen.

Questions:

1. Can you recall a time when a small thing that you said, or did, made an impact for good?

2. Have you the faith as small as a mustard seed? Use it and declare what God shows you.

3. What small thing will you do today for the Kingdom of God?

Printed in Great Britain
by Amazon